WHAT'S

FACE YOUR FEARS, IGNITE YOUR PASSION,

STOPPING

AND ACTIVATE YOUR DREAMS

YOU?

jane cook

Cover photo courtesy of Chanreas Phun and Jen Jewett.
Cover Design by John Credic Bruno of 100Covers.com
Illustrations & Artwork by Jane Cook
Interior Design by FormattedBooks.com

ISBN: 978-1-7352448-0-8 (Paperback)
ISBN: 978-1-7352448-2-2 (audiobook)

Library of Congress Registration Number / Date: TXu002207565 / 2020-07-14

DEDICATION

To my parents, Tom and Merle Grim,
who taught me to work, to love learning,
and always believed in me.

To my, husband, Kevin Cook, who
lets me be myself, follow my heart,
and allows me to try some crazy things,
even if it means failing, and even at a sacrifice
for himself.

To all the Creative World Changers who have
inspired me. You are my mentors. You are my heroes.

To you, Creative World Changer, _____,
may all of your creative dreams and visions
love, encourage, heal,
and light up the darkness in this big, beautiful world!

THANK YOU FOR PURCHASING

What's Stopping You?

All of the author's profits from this book support women
artisan groups around the world to create
sustainable income, freedom from poverty, undesirable work,
and oppression for themselves and their children.
Go to https://empoweredwomencreate.org
to learn more.

WHAT'S

FACE YOUR FEARS, IGNITE YOUR PASSION,

STOPPING

AND ACTIVATE YOUR DREAMS

YOU?

jane cook

Download the "What's Stopping You?"
Activation Companion Course
For FREE

Just to say thank you for buying my book, I would like to give you
the Activation Companion Course 100% FREE!
This course will enrich and deepen your activation to
see your dream to reality.
There are activation pdfs, bonus videos, audios, and artwork to
encourage you along the way.

Go to:
https://janecookcreate.teachable.com/p/activation-companion-course

CONTENTS

"THE SECRET INGREDIENT"

I ASK YOU to give me grace and liberty to include my guidance and interactions with God, Jesus, and the Holy Spirit in this book. May you be open to my honest sharing because you, yourself, are also on your journey with God, though you might not call Him that or recognize Him, but you have had those "coincidences," those crossroads, guidance, visions, dreams, or a "voice" or impression in your head regarding guidance, ideas, solutions, etc. You have experienced an "otherworldly" presence, a supernatural, or an unexplainable occurrence. The Father God, who is love, has lovingly encountered you many times and pursues you, as His child.

So, I ask that we share our stories together on this journey to be who we are designed to be, doing the awesome works we love and desire.

There is a completion, a wholeness only He can bring. I could not share my story or the lessons learned and wisdom gleaned apart from God, Creator, who designed us to do all that He created us for. Don't you hate it when someone gives you the recipe you asked for, but then you discover they left out the "secret ingredient," and your cake (or whatever) doesn't turn out as well? Something is missing! So, I could not give you this whole story and leave out the "secret ingredient." God is the "secret ingredient" for the full, abundant, creative life, knowing who we are and fulfilling our joy and purpose in love.

May He bless you and continue to draw you to Himself and equip you for every good work. He knows you. He made you. He loves you.

"Lord, you know everything there is to know about me.
You perceive every movement of my heart and soul,
and you understand my every thought before it even enters my mind.
You are so intimately aware of me, Lord.
You read my heart like an open book
and you know all the words I'm about to speak
before I even start a sentence!
You know every step I will take before my journey even begins.
You've gone into my future to prepare the way,
and in kindness you follow behind me
to spare me from the harm of my past.
With your hand of love upon my life,
you impart a blessing to me.
This is just too wonderful, deep, and incomprehensible!
Your understanding of me brings me wonder and strength.
Where could I go from your Spirit?
Where could I run and hide from your face?
If I go up to heaven, you're there!
If I go down to the realm of the dead, you're there too!
If I fly with wings into the shining dawn, you're there!
If I fly into the radiant sunset, you're there waiting!
Wherever I go, your hand will guide me;
your strength will empower me.
It's impossible to disappear from you
or to ask the darkness to hide me,
for your presence is everywhere, bringing light into my night.
There is no such thing as darkness with you.
The night, to you, is as bright as the day;
there's no difference between the two.
You formed my innermost being, shaping my delicate inside

and my intricate outside,
and wove them all together in my mother's womb.
I thank you, God, for making me so mysteriously complex!
Everything you do is marvelously breathtaking.
It simply amazes me to think about it!
How thoroughly you know me, Lord!
You even formed every bone in my body
when you created me in the secret place,
carefully, skillfully shaping me from nothing to something.
You saw who you created me to be before I became me!
Before I'd ever seen the light of day,
the number of days you planned for me
were already recorded in your book.
Every single moment you are thinking of me!
How precious and wonderful to consider
that you cherish me constantly in your every thought!
O God, your desires toward me are more
than the grains of sand on every shore!
When I awake each morning, you're still with me."
—*Psalm 139:1-18 TPT*

INTRODUCTION

I HAVE READ enough, watched enough, and listened to enough books, webinars, and podcasts. Enough! It's time to begin! Of course, I have fears and excuses. Who am I? What do I know? It's all been said. So many more people are more qualified than me. Would anyone even want to read what I write? Why would they? Do you ever have these thoughts? If you do, this book is for you! BUT everyone is just one, just a person seeking to find their way in the world and seeking to help others by what they find. I could keep waiting until I have more experience, more success, and more wisdom, but I think we all always feel like we are not yet prepared. At some point in time, we have to just DO IT. Go for it! Begin. Start. Something, anything, done is far more powerful than all the knowledge and ideas in the world that are still only "in the head" and not brought into being yet. It is time to bring those hidden visions, dreams, and ideas to life.

"The day before something is a breakthrough,
it's a crazy idea."
—*Peter Diamandis*

"God has given me this day to use it as I will.
I can waste it or use it for good, but what I do today is
important, because I am exchanging a day of my life for it."
—*Heartsill Wilson*

I will begin today. Who knows what this small, tiny beginning will bring or become? All that is required of me is that I give my '5 loaves and 2 fish' (John 6:9), that I give what is in my hands to Jesus, to others. That is all that He requires. He will multiply it. He is the God of abundance. I constantly remind myself that I 'have an abundance for every good work' (II Corinthians 9:8). I have enough time, enough resources, enough energy, enough!

I want this little book to inspire and encourage YOU to truly allow yourself to intentionally begin TODAY to step into YOUR dreams and visions—those things that are deep in your heart to do. What is it you care about? What are you passionate about? What do you love? What do you hate? What are you doing when time passes so quickly you are not even aware of it? I want to encourage you, dear one, to discover and believe that you are truly creative, created in the image of God, our Creator. He is amazingly creative, so creative that we are still discovering things He has created for us to find in this big, beautiful world!

Creativity is not only expressed in the arts, but in doing everything in our lives creatively. Can you believe that there is a creative solution for every problem you have and every problem on this earth?! What is stopping you? What is stopping me? Let's free ourselves, encourage each other, and collaborate with one another to see and to discover creativity that is in each one of us. Let's stop comparing ourselves with each other and feeling "less than" or "more than" others.

Do you realize that each and every one of us is truly one-of-a-kind? No one else is like you, has had the same experiences with the same people in the same circumstances, or sees the world the exact way that you do, with the same gifts and passions and callings. If we can just realize that all that is expected of us is to be ourselves, only ourselves, what freedom we would experience. We don't have to be like someone else or measure up to someone else. All you have to be, is you! Doesn't that take a load off your shoulders?!

I don't really like anything imitation, do you? Not chocolate, or diamonds, or gold, or silver, or even hamburger! And of course, none of us really like it when someone is not real to us. What a relief it is to realize that all we have to be is ourselves, created in the image of God with plans and purposes that He actually gave to us before we were even born.

"For we are His workmanship, created in
Christ Jesus for good works, which God prepared
beforehand so that we would walk in them."
—Ephesians 2:10

I am enough! You have created me, led me,
equipped and empowered me to do ALL
that You have called me to do.

We don't need to be like someone else. We don't want to be imitations of someone else and miss the opportunity to be the best at being ourselves. The world will miss you if you are not you! God showed me in 2015, while in the shower (Yup, I seem to hear well in there!), that I had some rejection and feelings of not being good enough. I heard Him in my mind say, "If I created you to be you, then all you have to be is you! Who are you trying to measure up to? No one. You are created to be you. You are free from comparison, competition, and expectations! Just be you because no one else can be!"

Be YOU because no one else can be!

God is so incredibly multifaceted and rich and deep that each person expresses a unique facet of God that no one else can. No one else can express Him the same precise way that you can. Wow! Isn't that amazing? We are created in the image of God, who is creative, therefore, we are creative! God calls into being the unseen, the invisible and makes it visible. We do too! We imagine things, and we create them. Every single thing in the world/universe was invisible/unseen at one time. Everything began as a thought, an idea, and then it became a reality—and not just physical things but the spiritual things as well. God inspires us and urges us to do all that He put in us to do! It's LIFE!

> *"There is a vitality, a life force, an energy, a quickening, that*
> *is translated through you into action, and because*
> *there is only one of you in all time,*
> *this expression is unique.*
> *And if you block it, it will never exist*
> *through any other medium and will be lost."*
> *—Martha Graham*

Always remember that your worth does not come from what you DO, it is in you from God, Your Creator. He loves you no matter what you do or don't do. You are so precious and valuable to Him. He simply extends an invitation to you to join Him in sharing love, joy, and peace to the world. You're DOING comes out of your BEING. And no, do not think, "Who am I to _____?!" If we think someone else can do it or is more qualified, etc., nothing gets done. Receive and accept your calling. That's all that you're responsible for. Arise! Shine! Fly! You don't have to wait to love and serve the others. Seek out the opportunities you have TODAY! What is stopping you? What is stopping me?

Don't let the word "passion" or "calling" scare you. Just pursue what interests you, what you are curious about, what you love to do, or a problem you want to see solved, or person you are motivated to help. You will pursue these things with passion and a sense of purpose naturally. What is it you are willing to invest in with your time, your energy, and your money? What are you willing to sacrifice for? What really gets you fired up or brings you joy?

Passion is just living through your heart. You feel fulfilled because you are where you're supposed to be, doing what you want to do with love, meaning, and purpose and creating good in the world. Stop agonizing about not being where you think you "should" be. You are not finished yet. You will grow and change. Just be you, right where you are. You can experience happiness and joy in the journey.

If you do not know what your dream is, please release the anxiety of not knowing or of not knowing how to do it, where, when, etc. Just breathe. Relax. You are on your own journey. This is not about me or about anyone else and what or how or where someone else is on their journey. This is all about you being open to actually hear yourself, to welcome your dream/vision to make itself known to you. Honor the dream/desire/vision that comes to you. Don't just "blow it off" like it is a fantasy, an impossibility. Don't shut it up. Let it speak to your heart. Let yourself dream it. Don't stop it. Hear what it is saying. Don't judge it. Be open to hear new ideas and possibilities as if there were no limit … there isn't! "All things are possible with God." You have a dream. You hear it. You see it, because it is there. It is there for a reason—YOU are to do it!

When you hear and see, treasure your dreams and ideas by recording them. Write them down in detail. You may want to even use a special journal or notebook just for your dreams and ideas. You can also write out your dreams in first person and in the present tense. Imagine and visualize what you are doing, how you are feeling, who you are with, etc. You might even want to record yourself speaking this first-person visualization of your dream/vision and listen to it often. Give yourself permission to pursue and move forward so that the dream becomes reality.

Allow this book to encourage you and give you some light or direction to move forward. It is your intention that draws to itself all that is needed. Always keep to your vision. Think, Speak, Act according to your vision. Do not be moved by what you see or whatever happens along the way. Walk in faith and release and trust that God is working with you and for your good. Avoid judging yourself or your progress because you do not know the chain of events that are in motion or what is happening that you cannot see. You cannot judge it. You do not have the perspective to see it correctly. Walk it on out in faith. Realize that today is the day to begin. Or if you have started and then have become discouraged; take courage and move forward. The act of picking up this book is evidence that you know you are called, and you are drawn to take action! Yes, there is timing, but because the dream has been revealed to you is evidence that it is to become a reality, and it is time to take a step toward your vision that is calling you today!

> *"The time is always now."*
> *—Peter Beard*

What's stopping you? Lies stop us when we believe them. Lies that say we cannot do something. What is it you need to believe about yourself to follow your dream/vision?

Write it down. "I need to believe that I am _____.
I can _____. I can _____."

What is it you need to believe to be a part of the solution?
What is it you need to do it?
"I believe I will _____.
I believe I have _____. I believe what I have is more than enough when given to God.

Let go of any lies or negative thoughts and replace them with truth. I once saw a picture when I was praying for a young teenage girl. It was a picture of a set, like a painting in a drama. The set looked so real, so lifelike, just like the lies she was believing about herself. Then I told her she could take the sword of the Spirit, which is the Word of God, Truth, and she could cut through the canvas set and see that it was indeed a lie, not reality, not truth. The truth indeed sets us free when our thoughts are revealed as lies.

"If you hear a voice within you say, 'you cannot paint,'
then by all means paint, and that voice will be silenced."
—Vincent Van Gogh

Don't listen to all the negative, critical questions, whether inside your own head or from others, because NO ONE knows what you can do. Only your Creator, who designed you to be you knows. And actually, what He wants for you is even bigger than what you are thinking for yourself! Isn't that wild?! You will also discover people will show up who do support you as you walk out the path of your dream. If you truly believed you could be successful, would you be worried or anxious? No, you would plan to succeed. What should you be doing right now if you are to be successful? You can do this. Step forward. Follow your heart, even if you don't know your final destination or exact path. There is always some unknown, some mystery. It's a journey, and the path will be opened up as you move along it.

Dreams
"I am exhilarated as I breathe in
the fresh air of a clear night
and see the stars blinking through the sky.
I will nurture the threads of dreams
incubating in my heart and mind
until they spring forth with energy
and excitement into their time."
—jane

My heart is to just be me—to be fully me—using the talents, gifts, purposes, and plans given to me. As the "Parable of the Talents" tells us, we are only accountable for what He gives us. What are we doing with what we have been given? The crazy, amazing thing is that there is NO limit to our potential. It is just up to us to use what we have. He's the one who multiplies. He gives more as we are faithful with what He has given us. He gives abundantly more!

Parable of the Talents

"For it is just like a man about to go on a journey, who called his own slaves and entrusted his possessions to them. To one he gave five talents, to another, two, and to another, one, each according to his own ability; and he went on his journey. Immediately the one who had received the five talents went and traded with them, and gained five more talents. In the same manner the one who had received the two talents gained two more. But he who received the one talent went away, and dug a hole in the ground and hid his master's money.

Now after a long time the master of those slaves came and settled accounts with them. The one who had received the five talents came up and brought five more talents, saying, 'Master, you entrusted five talents to me. See, I have gained five more talents.' His master said to him, 'Well done, good and faithful slave. You were faithful with a few things, I will put you in charge of many things; enter into the joy of your master.'

Also the one who had received the two talents came up and said, 'Master, you entrusted two talents to me. See, I have gained two more talents.' His master said to him, 'Well done, good and faithful slave. You were faithful with a few things, I will put you in charge of many things; enter into the joy of your master.'

And the one also who had received the one talent came up and said, 'Master, I knew you to be a hard man, reaping where you did not sow and gathering where you scattered no seed. And I was afraid, and went away and hid your talent in the ground. See, you have what is yours.'

But his master answered and said to him, 'You wicked, lazy slave, you knew that I reap where I did not sow and gather where I scattered no seed. Then you ought to have put my money in the bank, and on my arrival, I would have received my money back with interest. Therefore, take away the talent from him, and give it to the one who has the ten talents.'

> *For to everyone who has, more shall be given,*
> *and he will have an abundance; but from the one who does*
> *not have, even what he does have shall be taken away."*
> *—Matthew 25:14-29 NASB*

What is stopping you? What is stopping me? NO ONE can keep you from being you but YOU, not others, not the devil, only you. We will uncover the "stop signs" in our lives that are slowing us down and holding us back from living out the life of our dreams and all that is in our hearts. I believe your passion is just like mine. I want to be me and do what I am called to do. I want to see you discover your creativity and use it to make a difference in your world of influence. We will truly make a difference when we step out into our creativity in our families, work, cities, and nations!

So… Who am I to encourage and inspire you? I am actually a nobody, a regular, average person. I don't have great fame, fortune, or influence. I am unknown. I think that is why I finally decided to write this little book. I am a normal person, just like you, who has simply discovered the extraordinary in the ordinary! I am pursuing my dream. I am not an expert, hugely talented, successful, or wealthy. I am on a journey to see my dream become reality. Maybe it's time you heard this message from an unknown person for YOU to believe that YOU too can step into your dream, your vision, and your creativity—a gift to the world!

My background is pretty common and average. I was raised by wonderful parents. I did not experience major childhood trauma nor did I grow up with wealth and power. I grew up in the 60s-70s. My father taught industrial arts, gardened, and taught us how to camp and fish. He also remodeled old houses, so I did too. I learned many skills, but the most important thing that was ingrained in me was the belief that I could do whatever I put my mind to.

My mother was a secretary and became a nurse later in life. She sewed handmade clothes for my sisters and me, and gave us freedom to play and discover. I worked hard in school as a child but did not really stand out in any way as exceptional. I read ferociously, was adventurous, was creative, and loved to climb trees and ride bikes. I also loved to play music. I loved to learn. I still do.

I married a wonderful man and had two amazing daughters. I taught school and loved to create new and amazing experiences for my students. I still love researching and discovering new things and new ideas. I have done tons of different types of art over the years, such as painting, drawing, crochet, macramé, pottery, weaving, spinning wool, wood crafts, refinishing furniture, etc. I have loved and enjoyed every season of my life, but I always had a desire to help change the world in some way.

A vision, a dream began to develop in my heart, or maybe I should say that the passion began to reveal itself to me from deep within my heart. This is the journey I want to share with you, because I know that there is a vision, a dream, a passion, an idea, something in you that is revealing itself to you, and I want my little story to connect with you and encourage you to GO FOR IT! This book is about igniting you to take action to see your dream come into reality. May the action of simply reading this book be a step toward your dream and inspire you to much more!

"Dream lofty dreams, and as you dream,
so shall you become.
Your Vision is the promise of what you shall one day be.
Your ideal is the prophecy of what you shall
at last unveil ...
Dreams are the seedlings of realities."
—James Allen, As a Man Thinketh

"Start by doing what's necessary, then do what's possible;
and suddenly you are doing the impossible."
—Francis of Assisi

You know it's time! What's stopping you, World Changer?

Go to your free Activation Companion Course here:
https://janecookcreate.teachable.com/p/activation-companion-course

ACTIVATION
APPRECIATE YOURSELF–YOU ARE UNIQUE

1. How would you describe yourself?
2. What are your core beliefs/values?
3. What is your background? How were you raised?
4. What are your strengths?
5. What are your weaknesses?
6. What kind of friends do you have? Describe them.
7. Who do you like to be with? Why?
8. What do people ask your opinion about? Or want help with?
9. What do you love to do more than anything else?
10. What things do you often see that most people don't?
11. Make a list of 50 things you know how to do and have done in your life.
12. How do you want people to remember you?
13. Do you truly realize how unique and wonderful God created you?

ACTIVATION
BELIEVE

What do you need to believe about yourself to pursue your dream?

"I need to believe that I am _____. I can
_____. I can_____.

What is it you need to believe to be a part of the solutions? What is it
you need to do it?

"I believe I will _____.

I believe I have _____,
_____, and
_____.

I believe what I have is more than enough when given to God."

SECTION I

TIPS FOR THE JOURNEY

#1 BE CURIOUS ABOUT LOTS OF THINGS. READ A LOT. DO STUFF. YOU WILL MOST LIKELY HIT ON SOMETHING THAT INTRIGUES YOU MOST. PURSUE THAT! DO IT LOTS!

IN ALL THE "fearless play," I did discover an art medium that I liked using more than all the others—polymer clay. An art teacher friend gave me a book about it, and I discovered that artists were beginning to use it. One technique they were using was an ancient glass working technique called "canework" applied to polymer clay. Many of the ancient glass trade beads were made with this highly protected/guarded technique. This really caught my attention. I ran with it. The teachers liked my work and bought it. Most all of my other endeavors were appreciated as gifts, but no one had offered to buy before. LOL!

"I have no special talents.
I am only passionately curious."
—Albert Einstein

"A sense of curiosity is nature's original
school of education."
—Smiley Blanton

Reading lots of different types of things, experiencing different types of activities, having a variety of interests, taking walks, etc. is helpful in creativity. Einstein played the violin.[1] Beethoven took long vigorous walks.[2] Archimedes discovered buoyancy while taking a bath. Doing different things causes new connections in your brain and new pathways that can bring to light new ideas and connections between different things.

Once you see the solution or dream, then the most important thing to do is the "DO" part. Whatever is intriguing you, whatever your interests, do it LOTS!

> *"All of life is an experiment.*
> *The more experiments you make the better."*
> *—Ralph Wald Emerson*

> *"Lots of people want to be the noun*
> *without doing the verb."*
> *—Austin Kleon*

I want you to see some "steps" or "connections" in my story that are most likely similar to your story as we go along, because this book is really about YOUR story!

> *"For anyone trying to discern what to do with their life:*
> ***Pay Attention To What You Pay Attention To***.
> *That's pretty much all the information you need."*
> *—Amy Krouse Rosenthal*

ACTIVATION
WHAT IS YOUR DREAM?

Take a minute and answer these questions. Write them down. It will help slow you down to think about them.

1. What are you doing when you "could do it all day," and time passes before you know it?
2. What things upset or anger you?
3. What do you feel passionately about and could read or talk about forever?
4. What has been in your heart to do even as a child and has not gone away?
5. If you could be ANYTHING you want, with no worries or buts concerning finances, education, location, etc., what would you do?
6. If you could change one thing in the world, what would it be?
7. What are your favorite books and movies? Do they have anything in common?
8. Who do you look up to as your "hero" or someone you want to be like?
9. If your dream was fulfilled, what benefits would come into your life and the lives of others?
10. See your dream as it has already happened. Imagine what your life would look like if your dream was fulfilled. See the details and then describe a day in your new life.

Write your dream out in detail. Writing is powerful as you transform your dream into words. Write in first person, present tense. Writing in present tense wakes one up to the possibility of it actually happening!

How do you feel? What are your emotions? Who are you with? What are you doing? Where are you?

Write. Write. Write. Try to use all 5 senses. Then read it out loud. How does it make you feel? Record yourself reading your day in your new life when your dream is fulfilled. Listen to it frequently.

*"Faith claims a promise from
God then imagines a future in which it is fulfilled."*
—*Donna Partow*

Vision propels us to take the steps in the direction of our destiny. If you can't see it, you can't be it. Look by faith, and see what God has for you. Spy out the Promised Land. See it before you are there. See it before it is a reality. What good things does He have waiting for you there?

The answers to these questions are all clues to what is in your heart and what you are created/designed to do. Don't worry so much about "the calling" or "the one thing" you are meant to do. What is in your heart to do? What is your interest? What do you enjoy doing? Do what matters to you. It can make a difference. You can change people's lives. As you take action, more will come. Take some small step right now! Start! Begin! PUT THIS BOOK DOWN RIGHT NOW! Write down the answers to the questions. Write down what is in your heart. What is it that interests you? Take the first step of actually recognizing the possibility and write it down. Say it out loud. Now! What's stopping you?!

*"The place God calls you to is a place where your deep
gladness and the world's deep hunger meet."*
—*Frederick Buechner*

#2 INVEST IN YOUR INTEREST. LEARN FROM THE BEST.

I WANTED TO know more and more about polymer clay. I experimented and read. This was before there was much internet access or YouTube videos, etc. I spent the money to go to the cutting edge "Ravensdale Conference" in Washington for polymer clay artists, which connected me with the leading artists using polymer clay at the time and with other artists around the country who were also beginning to explore polymer clay.

The techniques I learned catapulted me ahead as I applied what I learned. I even traveled out of the country to attend workshops given by "artists" in this field of interest. This was time and money well-spent. I had many beautiful experiences that spurred me on creatively. Having a mentor or coach can help you grow quickly as you reap the benefit of their knowledge and experience. We are also living in an age of technology that helps us connect with teachers and leaders via videos, podcasts, audio, Facebook groups, and books. Take advantage of these opportunities. You will give yourself an edge by investing in yourself to go to conferences, workshops, etc. to learn from those in your field of interest, whether it is in business, the arts, ministry, etc.

ACTIVATION
INVEST IN YOUR DREAM & IN YOURSELF

1. What do you feel you need to research to know more about to follow your dream? Write it out. Take action today–Google, YouTube, or buy a book.

2. Who could help you learn what you need to know? Make a list or research to make a list and contact them.

3. Who could answer questions that you have? Make a list or research and contact them.

4. Keep your eyes and ears open. You will meet people and connect with people in unexpected ways. You will see opportunities to learn and connect with conferences, workshops, and learning opportunities. Be open to going. On-line is good, but in-person can be amazing. Be open.

5. Make a list of any opportunities you already are aware of and would like to consider. Pick at least one and make plans to do it.

6. Is there anything you need to learn about or how to use particular tools, equipment, computer, lap top, etc.? Make plans to purchase the equipment and begin learning to use the tools needed for your dream.

#3 TAKE THE NEXT STEP TO GIVE YOUR "GIFT" TO THE WORLD.

I TOOK THAT first scary step to share my work as I began to do craft shows. Then, as I progressed in skill and in development of my own unique ideas, I did art shows. I began to succeed and wanted to have more time to do more art. This success and desire caused me to risk another step. I actually asked my principal if I could teach half a day so that I could pursue my art work. Who does that?! He said, "Yes." As timing would have it, we were going into a 5th and 6th grade center, which would allow me to teach 6th grade art for half a day. This decision was a step to make more art and do more art shows. Our decisions shape our destiny. It is the little daily decisions that shape our lives.

ACTIVATION
TAKE A STEP

> ➤ Decide upon your first small step. It could be one of the things above. Do it.
> ➤ If you have done all of the above, write down your next step.
> ➤ Put it on your calendar, or even better, do it right now.
> ➤ Make the call. Write the email. Plan the trip.

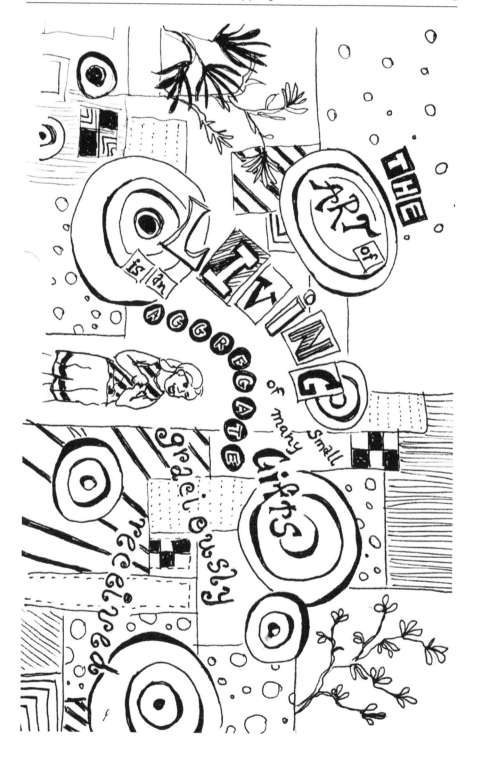

#4 AS YOU PROGRESS AND SEE SUCCESS, TAKE THE STEPS BEFORE YOU, EVEN IF IT LOOKS IMPOSSIBLE. ASK. SEEK IT OUT. PUSH ON THE DOOR.

THE HALF-DAY SPLIT between teaching and developing my artwork went well and gave me greater opportunity to devote more time to my art. I continued to learn new techniques as I grew in my level of expertise. Do not allow others to limit you or yourself. God designed you. Only He knows, and He says, "Yes!" (Remember Psalm 139). Nothing is impossible with God. If He put the desires, imagination, and dreams in us, would He not want us to pursue them and see them come to reality? Of course! Thank Him for the vision, the dream, the idea, and the revelation of the path to get there, even before you know it. He will show you as you ask, seek, and knock! You are on a journey. You don't really know where you are going exactly, but if you are open and take the steps before you, you will look back in wonder.

> *"You can't connect the dots looking forward;*
> *you can only connect them looking backward."*
> *—Steve Jobs*

The steps are truly divine, but in the midst of it, you may have no idea where the current situation may lead. Just keep going.

> *"Faith is taking the first step even when*
> *you don't see the whole staircase."*
> *—Martin Luther King*

#5 KEEP LEARNING. KEEP CONNECTING WITH OTHERS. BE OPEN TO THINKING "OUTSIDE THE BOX" OF WHAT IS BEING DONE. DEVELOP YOUR OWN UNIQUE IDEAS.

REALIZE "THE BOX" has been created by your past, experiences, teachers, environment, upbringing, etc. This box is actually constructed in your mind, and those around you have also constructed boxes for you and for themselves. How do you get out of the box? Your mind must be renewed. You must drop the old ways of thinking. Open your mind to new ways and different ways to do things.

I love to learn. I am curious and interested in so many things, maybe too many! I think I have my father to thank for this as well as my mother. They both were always busy making something or learning something new. They always supported me in my new ideas of what I wanted to learn or suggesting some of their own. I probably have a challenge in the opposite direction of wanting to do and to learn too many things!

Something that you can do to increase your creative thinking, to take risks, and to go "outside the box," is to do art exercises. You could art journal every day. How does art help you to think creatively about other areas and find creative solutions? Art teaches you to slow down and allow your right brain to click in. Our left brain is the verbal side, the linear thinking, one answer to a problem thinking side. The right brain is the visual thinking side, our subconscious, which has the ability to think divergently and to see many, many answers. When we take the time to develop our ability to think visually, we can learn to see beyond the natural. We can learn to imagine and accept ideas that might not make logical sense at first. When we take the time to draw or paint, we are developing our brain to see.

In art, we are also constantly making decisions of color, line, shape, and composition, developing a creative mindset to try things and risk to "see what would happen if." Art increases our ability to create options and to have a willingness to "fail" and to accept that things may turn out differently than we expected; but they can actually be better. We can discover new ideas. Art teaches us to try creative things and to take risks, to go outside the box. Art teaches us to ask, "What if?" These creative skills we learn as we develop our creative thinking/visual thinking can be applied to all parts of our lives. To "free up" your "outside the box" thinking skills, DO ART! Do it daily. Draw before you work. Doodle, draw, paint, move, and dance.

Lyn Lasneski teaches about "creative genius."[1] She has done research on genius and what it is and what the known geniuses had in common. They all saw solutions visually. The majority of them were artists. Einstein thought in pictures rather than words. His great breakthrough came from visual experiments performed in his head rather than the lab. For example, when he was 16 years old, he tried to imagine and picture in his mind what it would be like to ride alongside a light beam. He worked with this thought experiment for 10 years until he came up with the special theory of relativity.[2]

"I never came upon any of my discoveries
through the process of rational thinking."
—Albert Einstein

"Imagination is more important than knowledge.
For knowledge is limited to all we now know and
understand, while imagination embraces the entire world,
and all there ever will be to know and understand."
—Albert Einstein

I would highly recommend that you doodle, draw or paint daily, even if just for a short time. It will develop your ability to see, and this will carry over into whatever problems you are trying to solve. It will teach you how to think visually. You will begin to see "outside the box"—the "box" being past beliefs, mindsets, ideas, knowledge, and experiences. You will become a visual thinker. You will be in good company with Churchill[3], da Vinci[4], Einstein, and Pasteur. Your observation skills will increase. Your ability to see and imagine will be expanded. As Lyn would say, "You are a creative genius!"

"Learning is intimately connected to humility ... At the heart
of humility is an open-mindedness and open-heartedness,
with an inexhaustible appetite for illumination."
—Barnet Bain, The Book of Doing & Being

In my case, I had a convergence, a connection to an idea I had in college that did not quite work. I built a sculpture using PVC pipes in which I made some of them into flutes that could be removed from the sculpture and played. They did not play well, and they were ugly PVC pipe. BUT my mind connected that idea with my use of polymer clay and a possible way to make designs that could be applied to PVC pipe to make beautiful flutes! I researched the hole sizes, distance between the holes, and alignment to create flutes that would actually play a scale. BINGO! Unique, original idea. The polymer clay flutes opened new doors to new art shows, to a magazine article, to a calendar contest, and to being included in three polymer clay books.

Don't worry about the "how." These answers will come in the right time and way. Just do your part by believing. When you believe you are to move in a particular direction, things, people, books, places, TV shows, movies, devotions, scriptures, and conversations will start appearing and making connections with you to help you to move forward toward your vision/dream. The "unknown" has lots of opportunities waiting for you! Don't fear the "unknown." Move forward.

> *"The moment one definitely commits oneself,*
> *then Providence moves too.*
> *All sorts of things occur to help one that*
> *would never otherwise have occurred.*
> *A whole stream of events issue from the decision which*
> *no one could have dreamed would have come their way."*
> —W.H. Murray

Innovation truly comes in the work, as you work. Don't sit and wait for inspiration. Inspiration happens in the work, while you work. Start. Trust that you will experience a "convergence," a "connection" as well, and not just one time, but over and over to create new ideas. Be prepared. New ideas will come. You better keep a notebook by your bed!

ACTIVATION
BRAINSTORM—THINK OUTSIDE THE BOX

➤ Write down the problem you are wanting to solve or the idea you want to expand in the center of a piece of paper.

➤ Write down whatever you think you could do concerning the problem or idea. Write down anything and everything that comes to your mind. *Do not judge or screen* any thoughts or ideas or connections that come to your mind. Write them all down, no matter how silly or unreasonable. To think outside the box is to think creatively. You cannot think rationally, critically, judgmentally, or evaluate or analyze.

➤ Create. Play with ideas. Don't think. Don't care or be concerned if the ideas "make sense." You can look at them later, but you must allow your creative right side of the brain to have permission to play and to say whatever comes to mind. A tiny thought might spark something else and lead to an awesome idea.

➤ Write everything down around the central problem or dream idea.

➤ When you think you cannot think of any other ideas, press for at least 10-20 more ideas.

➤ Go deeper.

➤ Let the wild, outrageous, impossible, unbelievable ideas come out. Take a break.

➤ Come back and pick one idea you would like to pursue first and expand.

➤ Write it at the top of a clean sheet.

➤ Now look through all the other ideas and see if any connect with this idea and write them underneath.

➤ Creatively expand the idea with any ideas listed.

➤ Try another idea from the creative brainstorm list and do it again.

➤ Do this for as many of the ideas as you wish until you have an idea you want to work on.

➤ You can save the other ideas for a future project.

➤ Ask yourself questions. What if? What is it? What isn't it? How does this idea help, contribute, or improve others' lives?

#6 BE WILLING TO MAKE A GREATER COMMITMENT TO PURSUE YOUR CREATIVITY AND PASSION.

YES, AS YOU begin and take steps, you will come to a point where you will need to make a greater commitment to see that your dream/vision is fulfilled. The action you take reveals if you truly do believe in your vision. Your faith is revealed by your action. You can think about it, dream about it, prepare for it forever; but if you don't do it, you're not doing it!

A simple example of this is saying that you want to go on a trip, a vacation. Action reveals your belief about taking the trip. Your action is evidence that it is going to happen. You must mark your calendar, take off work, choose a destination, book a flight, reserve a place to stay, pack, and get on the plane!

In my life, the next step was another jump as I decided to go full-time into my art and left teaching in the public school system all together. I loved working as a full-time artist. It was great to have a flexible schedule for my girls and family. I had amazing favor at the arts shows, and my creative ideas continued. I loved my work so much.

Yet, around the 10-year mark, I felt a tug in my soul to connect with more people. I had an idea of opening a fresh juice and smoothie bar. The vision was clear, but the details were not working out. I felt I was just to continue doing my art, as it was not the right time. After another length of time, without really clear direction (just a desire to help people), I pressed on a possible door and picked up an application. Get ready for another connection, another convergence!

On my way home, I stopped at the local Christian Bookstore. It was closed. Surely not after 28 years? I made a call. Yes, they were moving. It was permanently closed. The thought ran through my mind, "Wow! Wouldn't that be cool to have a bookstore AND a Juice/Coffee Shop?!" But that wild thought was followed by the voice that says, "Sure, how could YOU do that? You've never done that before. You don't know anything about that. That would take a lot of money. Someone else will probably do it." Have you heard that voice before? Get ready for another connection, another convergence, and a BIG jump! I am a crazy book lover and reader, and have always been. I love books. I even love the smell of books, the feel of books. I love libraries and bookstores and discovering nooks with books.

I went home and proceeded to fill out the application for a job. My husband came home and asked me what I was doing. I continued to fill out the form as I told him about the application, and then I threw out a little "hook" without even looking at him.

"I saw that the bookstore closed permanently. Wouldn't that be cool to open one?"

I was shocked, yet a little hopeful, when I actually verbalized the possibility. I said it out loud. I kept writing with my head down.

My husband pressed, "So what are you doing?!" I repeated … He then took me by the shoulders, looked me in the eye, and said the most amazing thing to me, "No! What are you doing?! THAT would be perfect for you!" WHAT?!

ACTIVATION
GREATER COMMITMENT

➤ Are you at the point that you need to make a greater commitment to pursuing your dream?

➤ Why? Why not?

➤ What is it that needs to change?

➤ What is it that needs to be done to move forward?

➤ Remember that dreams only move into reality when action is taken.

#7 BE WILLING TO SHIFT GEARS WHEN OTHER CONVERGENCES HAPPEN. SOMETIMES WE JUST DO NOT KNOW HOW IT WILL ALL FIT TOGETHER, OR WHY.

I OPENED THE Oasis Christian Bookstore and Holy Grounds Coffee Shop. It was an amazing and beautiful time of connecting with lots of people and crazy accelerated learning in books, coffee, business, being an employer with staff, paperwork details, creativity and innovation, lots of technology, collaborations, etc. It was crazy and amazing. Working such extreme hours and days, I realized from the beginning that I would need to schedule and intentionally take time off to rest and refresh to keep up such a pace.

From the very beginning, even before the store opened as I waited for the remodeling to be completed, my wonderful, understanding husband sent me to the ocean. He knows that the ocean is a very special place to me. I always come back so refreshed and connected with God that we agreed that I should take a vacation each year, alone, as my spiritual retreat. I still do. Each time I have an amazing time of refreshment and of hearing God as I sit in the quiet that is found in the loud continuous crashing of the waves and look out over the vast expanse and soak in God's goodness and beauty.

Many times on these retreats to the ocean, I connected with women who are using their creativity, and my heart wanted to encourage them and help them in some way. My mind began to open up to the possibility of helping women with my creativity. This tug, desire, and passion increases as I step out and take trips and connect with people who are helping people around the world. I go to Africa, Haiti, the Bahamas, and Jamaica. I act to help dig wells, support a group of women artisans in Africa, collect and send tents to Haiti after returning home from a medical trip after the earthquake, etc. The desire to connect and help women to create sustainable income by sharing my creativity and encouraging theirs grows. How can I help? I remember lying on the floor of a hut in Africa after a time of worship under the stars, feeling in my heart that it was right. I wept and laughed, "But how could that be?! I am a wife, mother, mima, and owner of two businesses!"

ACTIVATION
DREAM/VISION BOARD COLLAGE

> ➤ Are things converging, coming together, to the vision?
> ➤ Are things shifting and looking differently than you expected?
> ➤ Can you remain open and still move forward into whatever step of action you see to do next?
> ➤ Write a statement of declaration: "I will _____. I will take the next step."
> ➤ Is there a fearless action you need to take? What is it?
> ➤ Read back over your visualization of your dream or listen to your recording of it.

Make a mixed-media dream/vision board collage:

> ➤ Cut out pictures related to your vision from magazines, the Internet, or your own photos and make into a collage representing your vision.
> ➤ You may want to add paint, words, and include a picture of yourself on the collage.
> ➤ Hang it up where you will see it daily.
> ➤ Pictures help you to visualize your dream. Pictures will speak to you consciously and subconsciously.

#8 CONTINUE TO BE OPEN AND TO FOLLOW YOUR HEART. TAKE ACTION ON YOUR IDEAS, EVEN WHEN YOU'RE NOT SURE HOW IT ALL FITS.

THAT FIRST MISSION trip to Africa in 2009 was literally life-changing. Besides recognizing the feeling in my very heart and soul of completion and fit, there was also the igniting of passion to continue to pursue the specifics of how I could truly help. When I returned home, I found myself overwhelmed with the goodness and the wealth of my life in the United States versus what I had seen and experienced as I walked the villages in Mozambique of mud huts without clean water wells, no provision for education, few opportunities to create sustainable income, etc. I also felt emotionally somewhat "guilty" for the wealth of my country by comparison.

I was then reminded of a scripture in Acts 17:26, "… determined our appointed times and the boundaries of our habitation." I felt God was saying that I was appointed this time in history, and He put me in the family, in the community, and in the country where He wanted me to be. The wealth? Not to feel guilty for it, but to be accountable for what I have been given, for what is in my hands, and to be faithful to use it for others. It was not given to me just for me! That perspective changed everything for me. I had always known that in my head, but now I had a heart experience with it, and it is a motivator for me to continue pursuing the vision, the passion.

I also remembered the story of Esther (in the book of Esther) who was chosen above many women to be queen to King Ahasuerus, who reigned from India to Ethiopia over 127 provinces. This happened during a time of persecution of Esther's people, the Jews. Later in time, Haman became aware that Esther was a Jew, and he wove a complex plot to have the Jews executed in the kingdom. Esther's uncle told Esther that she should go before the king to implore his favor for her people. He challenged her that perhaps she was "born for such a time as this." So, she went before the king with the attitude that "if I die, I die." Her courage did indeed save her people. So, just as Esther, we are also born "for such a time as this." We are each here for a reason, a purpose, which does indeed impact others!

As I took action by going on each trip and responded by doing what I could do, the vision began to be more and more clear that I wanted to help women around the world to create sustainable income for themselves and their children with creativity.

#9 BE OPEN FOR CHANGE AND BE WILLING TO TAKE FEARLESS ACTION TO PURSUE A NEW VISION.

I KEPT PURSUING this idea until one day in the shower (I think I hear better from God when I am not trying!). God spoke to me very clearly in my mind, "If you want to pursue that creative project, you must put down what is in your hands." What?! My first response was to weep. I loved the bookstore and coffee shop. I thought that I would do it forever, but I stopped crying in seconds ... How did I ever think I could seriously do both? I wanted to pursue the vision in my heart! Notice He did not say that I *had* to pursue the vision, but if I wanted to. I wanted to. My husband agreed.

I got the word out that the bookstore was for sale through my email list and Facebook. The next day I had two calls with people who seriously wanted to buy The Oasis Christian Bookstore. The second person worked out. I trained her the next month and turned it over the month after that. God truly confirmed this decision. It was a BIG leap of faith. Most of the time it is accomplished in small steps, but sometimes you need to make a big jump, a big step.

"Don't be afraid to take a big step
if one is indicated.
You can't cross a chasm in two small jumps."
—David Lloyd George,
Prime Minister Great Britain, 1916-1922

Jump In—Follow Your Heart
"In a glimpse of the mystery of truth,
we seek clarity and are humbled.
If we immerse ourselves in life,
With enthusiasm,
(Greek word means "one with the divine")
We find wholeness.
But we must jump in, risk immersion,
And not stand on the shore of rationalization."
—jane

There will be "unknowns"; we must look with eyes of ADVENTURE to move forward. One of my grandsons, as a toddler, loved to go on what he called an "adventure" in my flower beds. He loved to walk among the iris and day lilies and bushes that were as tall as or taller than he was. It was like a jungle to him. He loved to go on adventures!

I also liked going on adventures as a child. I liked to climb trees, play in hollow trees, investigate attics, and wander through vacant lots. I remember a summer spent in Minnesota going on an adventure. On my way to take some piano lessons, I would walk past an abandoned little church. I had to investigate. I was so intrigued with the boxes piled everywhere with just enough light from the stained-glass windows to see. There were old hymnals and songbooks along with an organ. It was an adventure. Still to this day, I love an adventure. I love to walk trails through the woods and nature. Even when I went to Fiji a few years ago, after a guide led a group of us to a beautiful waterfall, I dared to try to find the waterfall again by myself on morning hikes. It was amazing walking through the jungle to be rewarded with time to sit and just soak in the beautiful sound of the waterfall upon the rocks (So worth the hike!).

Adventures require curiosity and courage. Your journey as you follow your heart is an adventure. It is new. It is exciting. It is risky, but it is worth the risk. Staying where you are, as you are, is risky too! The word "adventure" comes from the Latin word "adventurus" meaning "a thing about to happen."

"Life is either a daring adventure or nothing."
—Helen Keller

ACTIVATION
DECREE

You may want to write your own fearless decree, but you can use this one to get you started!

Decree:

I am a daughter of the KING.

I have a place, a position in the Kingdom.

I am created in God's image with His creative energy and imagination of the unknown and the impossible.

I hear from God.

He directs my path.

He is the way.

I believe He has good plans and purposes for me to accomplish. I say yes!

I will not let fear, failure, overwhelm, discouragement, age, limitations, or procrastination stand in my way.

He has equipped me for every good work.

I have an abundance of seed to sow.

I have an abundance of everything I need including: Time, ideas, creativity, perseverance, ability & skill, opportunity, connections, timing, money, courage, power, strength, and vision!

I will seize the opportunities of the moment which will have an impact on the future.

I am changing the world.

I am making a difference.

#10 DON'T BE SHOCKED IF IT TAKES TIME TO FIND AND DEVELOP THE NEW VISION.

I WENT TO Africa for three months and connected with an artisan group of women there. (By the way, this was four years after my first trip to Africa when I did not know how it could possibly work out.) I expected to return again and continue to help them, but with a government situation concerning visas, I wasn't able to return at the time I thought that I would. I kept connecting with other opportunities as they opened up. I went to Thailand and Singapore and connected with a ministry helping women leave the sex industry to have income through a jewelry business. But the vision of working with women was not moving along as fast as I thought it would. I wrote the following in my journal in 2017:

"Can one be disciplined to pursue the 'vision'
though it seems to tarry?
Can one prepare and work day by day
to the potential for that day anyway?
O, God, frustration and overwhelm has led me
to discouragement and sluggishness.
Help me to be intentional. Help me to believe."

"Every great success is ultimately the triumph of persistence."
—Ralph Waldo Emerson

I turned my Austin Kleon calendar to September and it said, "JUST KEEP GOING" (https://austinkleon.com/). I was encouraged. In fact, I still have that 2017 calendar hanging up by my desk turned to

September. I never turned it, and it continues to inspire me! Difficulties can be opportunities, not obstacles, if you can just keep going to see the results.

"It is mission that inspires passion and zeal while vision provokes perseverance and sacrifice."
—Kris Vallotton, *Heavy Rain*

ACTIVATION
JUST KEEP GOING

➤ Make your own "Just Keep Going" sign.

➤ Paint, draw, or use markers to make your sign or make it on the computer.

➤ Hang it up where you work or where you will see it daily.

➤ Set a reminder on your phone, "Just Keep Going", that pops up weekly.

➤ Make it the wallpaper on your phone or laptop.

Remember to go to you FREE Activation Companion Course for pdfs for all activations plus bonus videos, pdfs, and audios!

#11 DON'T MISS THE WONDERFUL OPPORTUNITIES THAT COME YOUR WAY TO USE YOUR CREATIVITY WHILE YOU ARE ON THE JOURNEY TO "THE VISION." THESE OPPORTUNITIES ARE PRICELESS.

AFTER RETURNING FROM Africa, I connected with a friend from the UK that I had met in Africa who had started a ministry to children in Haiti. We both believed I was to come and help. I wanted to bring something creative to teach that would help the street boys to create sustainable income. I knew resources were limited. What could they do? What would work? As I prayed over the trip, a picture came to me from when I went to Haiti with a medical team right after the earthquake.

God asked me, "What do you see?"
"I see trash ... lots and lots of trash," I replied.

Then immediately Holy Spirit brought to mind the rag rugs my mother crocheted when I was growing up. Yes! That was it! From "Trash to Treasure," we could take the bags of t-shirts sold in the market from the U.S. to make the "plarn" to crochet rugs, mats, totes, etc.

I went to help her and worked with 25 street boys, ages 6-18 years old. We made cutters to cut the plastic soda bottles into strapping to use as cord to secure things or to repair the seats of chairs by weaving. I helped them with their coconut jewelry and gave them an art experience with painting. And they learned to crochet! All 25 boys learned to crochet from the youngest to the oldest. They made rugs and mats to sleep on, as well as totes and purses. They were amazing. I helped them to create product to create sustainable income. It was a beautiful opportunity.

More convergence continues with past interests and with teaching. I also made other connections with people of like mind and ministries while in Haiti. I hope to return there when the time is right. The hurricane prohibited my return when I had expected to that next year.

The connections with Iris Global, Heidi and Rolland Baker's ministry in Africa where I spent the two weeks of my first visit and the three months after I sold the store, not only connected me with a friend ministering in Haiti, but put me on the alumni's list to receive the Iris Global Alumni emails. There was a request from Cambodia for a jewelry designer to come and help start a program, a business, for women leaving the sex trade. Exactly my vision!

I have found it so interesting that all of life is a journey. Many times, we think we know where we are going but end up somewhere totally different than we expected. Other times, we do not know exactly where we are going. We are just headed in the right direction and blazing a new trail as we listen to our hearts and take courage to make decisions that take us toward the vision/dream. But the interesting thing that I have come to realize is that if I did know exactly where I was to go, I would just go straight there. I would take the most direct route in the shortest amount of time. But I would have missed all the points in between, the "scenic route," the experiences, hardships and difficulties, wonderful surprises, and joys that all go into what I have become. If we knew and took the direct route from point A to point Z and missed all the various experiences in between, we would not be the people we are! And we would most likely not be prepared or equipped for the purpose or dream of point Z, which actually I doubt that point Z is your final destination!

"Be open to paths not planned but unfolded
before you with possibility and discovery of
unexpected treasure found in the moment.
You are not lost."
—jane

ACTIVATION
DREAM JOURNEY POSTER

➤ Write your dream at the top.

➤ Write down when and how you became aware of this dream. Write down how you became convinced to pursue your dream.

➤ Write down all the steps you have taken so far.

➤ Remember every action, connection, opportunity, person, book, movie, miracle, etc. that has played a part in your journey to see your dream become reality.

➤ Be grateful for each experience, event, person, etc.

➤ Keep this poster up and add on to it all the amazing things that happen along the way.

➤ You can add dates if you wish.

➤ Be sure to add the unexpected opportunities that come as well.

➤ Use this to encourage yourself and to be grateful whenever you feel you are not making progress or are feeling discouraged.

#12 DON'T LET YOUR "LIMITATIONS" KEEP YOU FROM PURSUING YOUR VISION.

THE ONLY PROBLEM for me with the request for a jewelry designer to come to Cambodia was that the mission organization was requesting someone long term. I am married, with two daughters, seven grandkids, and care for some loved ones in their elderly years. I cannot go overseas long term. This is the prayer I wrote in my journal:

> *"God, forgive me for limiting You. Forgive me for not doing what you have clearly shown... looking at what I don't know. YOU know exactly what I need and when. Prepare my heart to receive greater revelation and glory to be able to carry the weight of all that you have called me to be and to do. I release You, Father, to give me revelation of exactly what YOU wish! I receive. My requests are so below what Your plan and will is. You desire to do exceedingly above and beyond all that I could ever ask, hope, think, or imagine! Implant Your Word in me, breath of God. Amen."*

So ... I could have just said, "It is not possible." Instead I chose to contact them and tell them what I COULD offer. I could come on a regular basis to teach, train, love, and support each year. I applied and interviewed. They invited me to come for an exploratory visit. I went to Cambodia for two weeks in February and got to see all the different work this ministry is doing and to explore the culture and the history of Cambodia.

My heart exploded for Cambodia. I was wrecked with the horrific history of the Khmer Rouge reign and the deaths of millions of people, the destruction of their country, the devastation of families, and the resulting heart wounds for those surviving. My heart also went out to the women and girls in the bars and brothels as I sat and talked with them. I gave each one a polymer clay heart I had made with the word "loved" stamped on the back. Such a simple little thing, once again I brought just "what was in my hand," and it was received. They loved them and pinned them on as I told them that they were loved. Connections were made for future relationships. It was an amazing trip. I was so "ignited" to have the opportunity to see the vision become a reality. It was agreed I would return in September for a two month stay to start the actual artisan group.

Don't let any limitation keep you from pursuing your dream. No one person can be good at everything. Turn whatever weakness you have into strengths, as they cause you to do things in a different, unique way or connect you with people who are gifted differently than you. Focus on what you have. Focus on your strengths.

"Again and again they limited God,
preventing Him from blessing them ..."
—Psalm 78:41 TPT

When we limit God with unbelief about what He can do, and what He can do through us, we cut off His blessings. We prevent Him from being able to bless us. After I read this scripture, I pondered it in relation to seeing my dream come to reality. I prayed:

> *"I trust You, O God. You will lead me and show me. You will open the way before me. I do not want to limit You by thinking this dream is 'too big' or 'too much' for me. YOU are able! YOU are much more, above and beyond able! Do in me and through me all you desire. Amen."*

Provision may not be seen where you are standing at the moment, but it will be in front of you, where you are about to go. Don't be limited by externals such as your resources, education, environment, past, money, etc. Agree with God's direction for you. Agree with His word, His promises.

> *"The success of our lives is more determined*
> *by our imagination than our circumstances."*
> *—Richard Paul Evans*

> *"A warrior mindset is always focused on victory.*
> *It allows no possibility of defeat.*
> *It does not retreat. It stands under extreme pressure.*
> *It advances by God's permission. You already have the*
> *victory. Abiding in Christ is the key to experience it."*
> *—Graham Cooke*

#13 VISION COMES WITH SACRIFICE (FINANCIAL, TIME, AND COMFORT), NOT ONLY FOR YOU, BUT FOR YOUR FAMILY.

I HAVE SUCH a precious family. We are very close. When I am gone, it is a sacrifice for my husband, my daughters, and my grandkids, as well as others who depend on me. So, they have to work together to cover lots of situations and times that I normally would have. Their love and sacrifice make it possible for me to go. There is also the money commitment, but I believe the scripture that says that we have an "abundance for every good work." My finances and the startup cost for the artisan business came together as it was needed. My return trip to Cambodia was in September for two months and came around quickly. I arrived with two 50-pound suitcases of art supplies and tools and a carry-on of personal items. All the details for lodging and transportation came together and worked out.

Provision is not where you are at the moment, but where you are going. I stepped out in faith on the "water" of truth, which is in fact a "rock" that according to II Corinthians says that I "have an abundance (more than I need)" for every good work!

> "And God is able to make all grace abound to you, so that always having all sufficiency in everything, you may have an abundance for every good deed; as it is written, 'He scattered abroad, he gave to the poor, His righteousness endures forever.' Now He who supplies seed to the sower and bread for food will supply and multiply your

seed for sowing and increase the harvest of your righteousness;
you will be enriched in everything for all liberality,
which through us is producing thanksgiving to God."
—*II Corinthians 9:8-11 NASB*

"Poverty is accepting a limitation
and being governed by lack."
—Graham Cooke

ACTIVATION
APPRECIATE

> Remember to appreciate your family. They are also affected by what you are doing.
> Thank them. Be sure to make time to be with them.
> Keep your balance.
> Make a list of all the people who have encouraged and supported you along the way.
> Think of a creative project you could do for each one to show your love and gratitude.
> Write it down next to their name and when you will do it.
> Do it.

#14 YOUR VISION IS NOT JUST YOUR OWN, BUT WILL INCLUDE MANY OTHERS THE BIGGER IT IS. THEREIN IS THE DELIGHT AND THE DIFFICULTY.

AFTER I ARRIVED, we purchased tables and set the studio up in an apartment close to the red-light district, behind the Royal Palace. Getting an oven that holds the temperature proved to be a challenge. Our first woman in the program is absolutely amazing. She was so excited to have the opportunity for a new job. She has proved to be a wonderful worker and artist. She has two children who are able to go to school now. The precious little girl asked her mother a question a week or so after her new employment.

"Mommy, do you like your new job? Because I sure do!"

"Why do YOU like my new job?"

"Because you are home with me at night to hold me and snuggle with me when I go to sleep."

I wept. This was the vision I had to help women to be empowered by creativity to create sustainable income for themselves and their children, and to create an artisan group of women who are creating beautiful things to share with the world while helping each other to heal and to prosper.

We were also blessed with a young woman to translate for us. She is key to the whole project. She is full of kindness and patience. Everything about the work with the girls was amazing and gave me such joy to finally see the passion, the vision become reality. Yet, in all the good there seemed to be an undercurrent of confusion or lack of communication about what I was to do and what some of the team were told or not told. So, in the midst of beautiful, wonderful things happening and the beautiful unity of vision, there can still be confusion and threat of disunity.

"Where no oxen are, the manger is clean, but
MUCH revenue comes by the strength of the ox."
—Proverbs 14:4

Fruitfulness and productivity are messy and require much work. Be prepared to search out and seek what the problems are and how to circumvent and diffuse them with love, compassion, and understanding. Be prepared to be humble. The vision/dream is bigger than you think.

"Never doubt God's mighty power to work in you and
accomplish all this. He will achieve infinitely more than your
greatest request, your most unbelievable dream, and exceed
your wildest imagination! He will outdo them all, for his
miraculous power constantly energizes you."
—Ephesians 3:20 TPT

"Now to Him who is able to [carry out His purpose and] do
superabundantly more than all that we dare ask or think [infinitely
beyond our greatest prayers, hopes, or dreams], according to
His power that is at work within us."
—Ephesians 3:20 AMP

"Now to Him who is able to [carry out His purpose and]
do superabundantly more than all that we dare ask or think
[infinitely beyond our greatest prayers, hopes, or dreams],
according to His power that is at work within us."
—Ephesians 3:20 NASB

Wow! I love that verse!

ACTIVATION
OTHERS

➤ Are you working with others to see your dream come to fruition?

➤ How is that going? Are there difficulties?

➤ Be prepared to search out the problems with love, compassion, understanding, and humility.

➤ Talk to God and ask Him about any issues you are having with others.

➤ He has the wisdom and the love for you to have for any situation.

#15 STUFF HAPPENS. CAN YOU KEEP GOING? P.S. BE SURE TO PURCHASE MEDICAL INSURANCE WHEN TRAVELING OVERSEAS.

THE SECOND WEEK I was there, I got really, really sick to my stomach, bloated, and feverish. I couldn't even lift my head or sit up. Now that is NOT what you want to do when you have sacrificed and paid the price to finally be there and do what you feel called to do. I hated to call in sick. Thankfully, we had had a week together, and the girls could work on the things we had started. Finally, after I continued to be sick for two days and with increasing excruciating pain, I went to a doctor, no conclusion, phone call to doctor the next day, instructions to get a sonogram, then instructions to go straight to the hospital, and an hour ride through traffic in a rickshaw to the hospital. I was so grateful to be in Phnom Penh, a big city, with a great hospital. They sent me straight back to the ER, IV, CT scan, etc. The doctor spoke good English but wanted to be sure I understood the seriousness of the situation, so he drew a picture for me. My appendix had ruptured, and I was full of infection and nasty business. He wanted to operate within the hour. I had to prepay a deposit of $6,000 until the insurance could kick in. I was thankful our credit card could cover it.

"Adversity introduces us to ourselves."
—Jim Kouzes

On the spiritual side of the situation, I can honestly say that God truly showed up for me and gave me a gift of His peace. It was a serious situation in a foreign country without my family, but God is God everywhere, and

He is with me everywhere and always. His peace was so strong on me, though in pain and aware, I was not afraid and had no thought of dying. The surgery was performed at midnight. The team called my family, but since I didn't have my phone when I woke up, I could not call them until the next day. This was a stress and stretch for my family. Besides their sacrifice of letting me go, caring for others I care for in my place, and all the details, they also had to go through this time of separation at a time of crisis, not knowing for sure what was going on or being able to help me and be with me.

"If you want a happy ending, that depends,
of course, where you stop your story."
—Orson Wells

The director of the ministry came in the next day and told me that if I wanted to go home when able, they would all understand. My passion rose up from deep inside me and I said, "Heck, No! I will not let this affliction of the devil keep me from doing what is in my heart that I came here to do. I will do whatever I can do in my weakness. I will not let him steal any more than he already has!"

Yes! You will have adversity. Yes, you will have "stuff" happen in the midst of your dreams coming to fruition (hopefully not a ruptured appendix or a poisonous spider bite like I had in Africa), but you must make the choice to keep going no matter the difficulties, whether they be physical, emotional, spiritual, and/or relational. You can choose how you will go through the difficulty—with grace and humility, patience and strength, hope and faith, or not. You can also choose to discover and allow something good to come out of the adversity and during the adversity.

I was in the hospital for seven days and was so sick, I could hardly talk. I had so many wonderful team members who came by to check on me. I simply asked them to talk and to excuse me. I wanted to hear their stories on where they came from and how they ended up in Cambodia. I was so blessed. It gave me such joy to hear their beautiful stories about how God had pursued them and how they discovered their passion and desire to come to Cambodia and help people. It was a precious, sacred time of connecting and bonding together that would not have been possible otherwise.

"Rather than waiting to be rescued
from the hard journey, continue on,
just as rivers that come together
and merge into the sea, so will you. Keep on.
No matter the path."
—jane

"Much good work is lost for the
lack of a little more."
—E.H. Harriman

ACTIVATION
I CAN DO ALL THINGS

> Create a reminder and encouraging sign of Philippians 4:13
  "I can do all things through Christ who strengthens me."
> Cover a sheet of paper with paint, collage, stencils etc.
> Then print, paint, stamp, or collage the words of Philippians 4:13
  and add to the mixed-media piece.

#16 NO MATTER HOW BUSY YOU ARE, MAKE TIME FOR YOUR MORNING TIME OF QUIET AND REFLECTION TO CONNECT WITH GOD AND WITH YOURSELF. HE WILL SURELY BE YOUR GUIDE AND YOUR STRENGTH.

THE RELATIONAL ISSUES may be the most surprising to experience, yet just as working together as a team can always have its challenges, you may think that when you are pursuing a vision/dream that you will be exempt from these natural difficulties that happen as new projects are being developed. I would say, "Not!" Be prepared to work through and handle these delicate new relationships with grace and love.

My discovery was that the Holy Spirit showed me specific areas of confusion and concern so that I could shift and adjust to be sensitive to these. This actually prevented offense and issues that could have caused the project to fail right out of the gate. If I had not been in the habit of getting up early every morning to spend this time of prayer, reflection, and journaling, I might not have made the time in Cambodia, but I did. God spoke to me in my mind, through His Word, through a devotional book that I brought, and as I journaled. I could not do this alone, and you don't have to either! I cannot do my dream/vision by myself and neither can you. We need people and we need God, the one who gave it to us in the first place, who promises to go with us and to finish the good work He started in us.

> "In the Presence of God is the only way to fulfill our
> God-given destinies. Keys to our callings are released
> when we spend time there."
> —Heidi Baker

"He is our true source of life: More is accomplished
by spending time in God's Presence
than by doing anything else ...
and the secret to sustainability is the secret place."
—Heidi Baker

"The rest we seek is not a rejuvenation of our energy;
it is the exchange of energy; our life for God's, through
which the vessel of our humanity is filled with the Divine
Presence and all sufficiency of Christ Himself."
—Francis Frangipane

"Seeing is about receiving, the way early photographs would receive
images from the world, and in the dark they would slowly develop.
This is why stillness and quiet allow
what we see and receive to develop
within us into patterns of insight and understanding.
And reflection and expressing through writing
is a timeless way of developing
what we see and receive."
—Mark Nepo

Journaling and taking time to be quiet and still to listen and to experience God's presence each morning has truly been my strength and source of peace, wisdom, joy, love, and guidance. Time with God is a must for me. If you are not in the habit of a daily morning time, you may want to begin and make it part of your daily routine. The activations have lots of ideas and activities for your time with God, but the main thing is to just get quiet and still enough to listen!

"The secret of your future is hidden in your daily routine."
—Mike Murdock

Journal your dreams. Be ready to write things down first thing in the morning so that you don't forget the insights, ideas, and dreams that you have. You will want to refer back to your journal to remember them. Your journal will also encourage you during times of confusion and difficulty. You can review and reread your entries about your successes, changes, errors, dreams, ideas, solutions, etc. You will also want to journal your ideas, even if they seem random and don't seem to connect with the moment. You may be busy about your day and can record the ideas on your phone or in the Evernote app. (This is an amazing app for organizing your notes—typed, copied, or audio—into categories with tags so you can find them later.)

I used to think that I could/would remember ideas that came to me, but learned I didn't! I write or record an idea as soon as I receive it. You may want to keep different journals/notebooks for different purposes. I have actually journaled since I was in 1st grade. I like to write! It helps me process things. I have several notebooks for personal life and work: a daily journal, book notes, dreams and spiritual revelations, ideas for my art work, ideas to teach the artisan women groups, marketing ideas, and book ideas. These notebooks come in handy to review and remember treasured ideas, revelations, and insights. Reviewing my notes can trigger new ideas and projects. In the process of writing this book, I went from notebooks to using index cards so I could divide them up into the specific topics and organize them to add into the "in-process book." The index cards can be moved around as needed.

To be healthy and creative with energy, we also need to give our brains a rest and use the right side. I have found that the daily, simple, repetitive tasks, such as showering, washing dishes, driving, walking, gardening, crochet, and even napping give the right brain a chance to come up with answers, ideas, and dreams that the left brain drowns out with its verbal chatter. I think that is why I also seem to have "revelations" and ideas right when I wake up in the morning, because my mind is quiet, and I can hear.

*"The body benefits from movement, and
the mind benefits from stillness."*
—Sakyong Mipham

Besides caring for yourself spiritually and emotionally, you also need to care for your body. We know that we need to eat healthy, exercise/move, and get adequate sleep, but do we?! If we want to "go the distance" and accomplish all that God has planned for us, we need to take care of our body.

"If you don't take care of your body, where will you live?"
—unknown

*"None of that other stuff is going to work if the animal
that you live in is a broke-down mess."*
—Elizabeth Gilbert

If your body is worn out, sick, and weak, it will be difficult to pursue your dream. Set your exercise, diet, and personal care routines. If you feel resistance, set a strategy of just one small step. One step that is easy for you to do … Like putting on your tennis shoes, or not buying junk food, or scheduling a massage, or going on a walk. With consistency, you will see these areas turn around in your life. And watch what you say to yourself. Speak kindly and with love to yourself! No more condemnation and judgment and criticism, just move forward in faith and freedom.

I can give you an example. After the ruptured appendix and emergency surgery and hurting my foot by kicking a concrete step, my exercise dropped down to very, very little. When I got home from Cambodia, some kind of trigger clicked on after being without certain foods, and I ate more than I needed and more junk food. Due to some family health issues and the care I needed to provide, my stress levels were high and activity levels were low. The result? An additional 20 pounds. Frustration and depression make it difficult to have the energy needed to make a change, but small steps do work.

One thing that has worked well for me to increase movement has been to use the Be Focused app. I get so engrossed in working on the computer or on my artwork that I don't move for hours. I set the app for an hour. It goes off, and I get up and move, dance, jump around, or whatever for five minutes, then reset. If I continue to do this every day, those five-minute breaks are bound to add up on top of the mini workout I do every morning! You will come up with your own strategies. The main thing is to do it.

The other thing that I am doing is keeping my focus on the positive process—eating healthy, moving, making time for rest and walks, etc.— NOT on the negative of "Jane, you need to lose 20 lbs." I have actually had to move the scale to break the pattern of berating myself for the extra pounds. I am feeling so much better and am excited to see how the change of focus and positivity affects my body as well. I will continue to focus on process and trust results will follow.

Care for self increases longevity. I want to keep fit for all the wonderful adventures ahead! To breathe. To walk. To laugh. To clean and organize my space. To think clearly and to be ready to work. To make time for family and friends. To write. To play. To make music. I believe that "my times are in His hands" (Psalm 31:15), but I want to do my part to care for the vessel He has given me while on this earth. I want to live every year, week, day, and moment of life that He has planned for me. I don't want to miss out on a thing by cutting it short due to my own negligence. It really bothered me when I turned 50. I had a choice—to get depressed and think that I was old or to "rise up on eagle's wings" (Isaiah 40:31) and accomplish more and enjoy more in the second half of my life, even more than the first!

"Work when there is work to do,
Rest when you are tired,
One thing done in Peace will most likely
be better than ten things done in panic...
I am not a hero if I deny rest;
I am only tired."
—Susan McHenry

Your body, soul, and spirit all need to be cared for. You need to schedule time to fill yourself up. Create a daily routine that nurtures you—body, soul, and spirit. Take the time to do the things you enjoy for your soul. Keep your heart clear. Forgive and love. Schedule time to connect with God and with yourself for your spirit. Listen. Pray. Write. Journal. Read. Soak. Meditate. Care for your vessel. All of you matters. All of you has an effect on the ultimate goals and purposes for your life. It's absolutely necessary to care for each part of you, because it is the only way you can completely express your gifts and give of yourself fully. Nourish yourself and your dreams. What inspires you is not selfish or an extra. What inspires you is necessary! It is necessary to be able to give your best self. Do whatever is nourishing for you. Ordinary things can be nourishing: a walk in nature, a laugh with the kids or grandkids, a soak in a hot bath, a nap with your comfy, soft blanket, etc. When you rest, refresh, refuel, you may be surprised that insight may come when you get away from work. Love. Live. Be. Breathe.

> *"You must be personally sustainable to do the work of change. Cherish your precious, worthy self."*
> —Gail Larsen

Care for yourself so you can care for others. You want your work to be sustainable and it can only be when *you* are.

"Every happening, great and small, is a parable whereby God speaks to us, and the ART of life is to get the MESSAGE."

Malcolm Muggeridge

Spinning
"Wow ... My head is spinning
Routines are disturbed
Everything is stretched.
I am grateful I can help,
But it comes with a price,
A sacrifice of something,
Of value given—my time,
My life.
Nothing is left untouched
Even the very core of my days—
My quiet time with You,
The early morning hours of
Solitude, reflection, connections, and revelation,
Projects, business, and art
Is unavailable ...
This a season of great need in their lives ...
I just need to curl up in Your hand,
The hand in which no one can snatch me out of, and rest.
I am weary.
God, how can I navigate this time?
It's like driving with the brakes on.
I have so much I want to do and
To accomplish.
Yet I cannot ignore the need before me.
I thank You for Your Grace and Your Love.
I drink deeply from Your Spring.
Refresh me. Renew me.
Show me how to navigate this time—well."
—jane, 8/10/19

David, before he became King of Israel, found himself in many difficult situations. At one point, David and his men offered to give their aid in a war. When they returned, they found that their own families had been taken, along with all their belongings, and their homes were burned.

The men were angry at David, their leader, for having them leave their homes to fight a battle for another people, and they wanted to kill him (I Samuel 30). But David strengthened himself in the Lord his God. David chose to find strength over giving in to discouragement. He chose to ask the Lord for wisdom about what to do. Like David, when we encounter difficulties, and we feel like we are all alone, we must go to God. We can do all things through Christ who strengthens us! He will give us wisdom and direction.

God told David to pursue the ones who took their families and destroyed their homes, that they would overtake them and rescue all those who were taken. David did. The families were recovered, along with all of their belongings. Victory began with a choice of *who* to turn to and *what* to look at—the problem or God? He had to change his heart and take dominion over his emotions and make them line up with God's Word. We can do this, too, in our daily lives by meditating on what God says in His written word, the Bible, and also by listening to Him speak to us. We want to meditate on His way, His solution, and His wisdom in every situation rather than to "meditate" on the negative and the problem creating worry. Worry is meditation on the negative, the bad, the wrong, and fear. It is actually visualizing and seeing it happen to you. Choose to pray the positive and the truth. Speak the positive and agree with God's Word. Visualize and focus on the good and what He says. In meditation, we focus on God's love and His Presence.

Daniel is another example of overcoming great difficulty by keeping faith in God. His country and people were taken into slavery. He served a pagan king. He lived in an oppressed environment, yet he had a daily time of prayer with God, and he impacted the nation for good. Evil men connived a scheme against Daniel to trap him by a law that made it illegal to pray to any god but the king. They knew that Daniel prayed daily to his God. When Daniel was found praying to God, he was thrown into the lions' den. The king anxiously waited all night to see if Daniel's God could save him. Daniel, even in the lions' den, in darkness, experienced peace and trust in God. The angels protected him. Daniel's God did save him. Even when things may get very dark and it seems injustice has won, we can keep our hope and faith in God who is able to save us and come to our aid in any situation we may find ourselves in. Daniel had an ongoing, daily relationship with God. This is my desire also, to know God and to be ready for challenges and even life-threatening situations.

As you begin your day with intention, you will want to end your day with intention as well. End your day with remembering all the good things of the day, all the positives. Incorporate gratefulness into your daily routine. Write/declare your gratefulness in the morning and before you go to sleep at night. Gratefulness opens your eyes to what you have and your heart to receive even more. Record them in your journal and thank God for them out loud. I have made a pact to be more grateful and thankful this year and actually express it. My daughters and my sister also decided to be more intentionally grateful this year. We decided to create a chat group in which we each share three things we are thankful for each day. It has been a great reminder. We also speak them out loud. It's amazing how that simple thing of speaking it out of your mouth connects your heart in a special way, and it becomes thanksgiving to God, which brings His presence. We know that being more grateful will surely make a difference in us and for those around us.

Before bed, you may want to plan the one focus for tomorrow. I have found lists to be overwhelming (other than to look at it to know what I want to focus on for the day and then lay it aside). Lists leave me feeling like I failed by not completing everything every day, but having a focus or intention that I want to work on, not necessarily finish, has made it much simpler and more positive for me. Focusing on the process, on a piece of the process, has helped me and freed me. It seems that I am truly knocking out the most important things better, rather than procrastinating by doing things that really don't amount to much. (Which is my tendency when I am overwhelmed.)

There are many ideas on daily routines and times with God, contemplation, and meditation. I will give you a few ideas, but remember that the most important thing is that you just take a few moments to start your day to get quiet and check in with yourself and connect with God. You need a moment to quiet yourself, listen, reflect, and to breathe. This time will have a dynamic affect upon your attitude, perspective and wisdom for the day. You will face your day more prepared.

ACTIVATION
BODY–SOUL–SPIRIT

➤ Be sure to check in with yourself. ALL of you needs care.

➤ Walking daily is good for Body, Soul, and Spirit. Walking can be "moving meditation."

Solvitur ambulande or it is solved by walking.
—St. Augustine

➤ List how you care for your body.

➤ List things you need to do. Plan to do it.

➤ Check in with your Soul, your emotions and relationships. Are you doing things that fill you up and refresh you? Are you being grateful and kind to yourself?

➤ Are you practicing kind and positive self-talk? Monitor what you say to yourself in a day. How would you speak to a child/ a friend/ or a grandchild? Honor and love yourself. Speak kindly and gently to yourself. Encourage yourself. Speak to yourself out loud.

➤ Journaling in the mornings is really helpful to put you in touch with yourself and to clear out any clutter and issues.

➤ Are there any changes or additions needed here?

ACTIVATION
ASK & LISTEN

This is 2-way communication.

Sit quietly and comfortably. Breathe. Release all worries and cares to God. Pray for a cleansing of your thoughts and ask forgiveness for anything that arises. Ask the Holy Spirit to fill your mind. Release the tension in your muscles. Quiet your mind. If something keeps swirling that you need to do later write it down.

After you are quiet, ask God a question, as simple as, "What do You think about me?" "Do You love me?" "What do You want to say to me?" or "What do You want to tell me today?"

Wait quietly. God speaks in thoughts and pictures. Write down in your journal whatever small impression or picture comes to your mind. Just start writing and keep writing whatever is flowing. He is speaking to you. When there are no more thoughts, stop, and read it to yourself out loud. Surprised? God wants to speak to you. He always speaks positively and with love. Negative, condemning thoughts are not from God.

Here is an example: One morning, I asked God, "Am I crazy to try to write this book?" He replied, "Jane, you are my precious daughter. Thoughts that come to you are from Me. My creativity, My thoughts and desires are within you. Why are you worrying? You are doubting your ability. This is not about ability, this is about releasing what is in you to the world in whatever format or way you choose! Leave the results to Me. I am the great "connector." I know who needs what and when. I hear the prayers that are being prayed for the solutions you can give. Continue to believe and stand on My ability to complete the good work I started in You. I have chosen you. You have a place and a purpose now and in eternity. You belong.

Love, Your Heavenly Father"

ACTIVATION
S.O.A.P.

I ran across this simple way to focus and to hear God speak through Scripture. I believe the most important thing about reading the Bible is to hear God and to encounter God through the Scripture. Our devotional/ morning time is not about an in-depth study of the Bible, although that is good, but this time is to meet God in His Word. So instead of having a preset idea of how much you should read, just begin to read. (I recommend starting with the book of John.) Read until a verse or a word "pops out" to you, or when you have a question or something catches your attention then stop. The Holy Spirit is highlighting something to you about that verse or verses on purpose to speak to you. So stop. Don't keep going and miss the opportunity. Ask Him what He is saying. You will want to record what He says in your journal so that you don't forget it and you can apply it to your life.

Here is the simple format:

S – is the Scripture. Write out the scripture that you are focusing on.
O – is Observation. What are you observing about this verse? What caught your attention?
Why? What is happening? Write down anything else that you notice.
A – is Application. What can you apply to your own life from this observation? What can you do? How can you respond? What is God speaking to you through this verse?
P – is Prayer. Write a prayer concerning this revelation in response to God's Word to you.
Receive what He has for you.

(Go to you FREE Activation Companion Course to see an example.)

ACTIVATION
YOU ARE THERE

Whatever scripture you are reading in the Bible, visualize/imagine yourself there in the story.

You are there. What are you doing? What is happening? How do you respond? Does God/Jesus speak to you? What does He say? What do you say? What is the conversation? Write down what you experience. Journal what you learn or hear through this experience.

ACTIVATION
MEDITATE ON SCRIPTURE

Meditation means to murmur, mutter, ponder, imagine. We fill our minds with God's Word and empty our minds of worry and care. We focus on Jesus and not on problems. Romans 12:2 says, *"Do not be conformed to this world, but be transformed by the renewing of your mind, that you might prove what the will of God is, that which is good and acceptable and perfect."*

There are a variety of ways to meditate. Select a meaningful scripture that God has led you to and that speaks something powerful to you. It could be a promise, a verse, or as long as a chapter.

1. Write it down
2. Speak it out loud. You could also record yourself reading the scripture.
3. Think about what it means and what God is saying to you through it.
4. Speak it in 1ˢᵗ person. Speak it with your name in it.
    Example: Psalm 1:1-3

> *"How blessed is the man who does not walk*
> *in the counsel of the wicked,*
> *Nor stand in the path of sinners,*
> *Nor sit in the seat of scoffers!*
> ² *But his delight is in the law of the LORD,*
> *And in His law he meditates day and night.*
> ³ *He will be like a tree firmly planted by streams of water,*
> *Which yields its fruit in its season*
> *And its leaf does not wither;*
> *And in whatever he does, he prospers." NASB*

How blessed am I. I do not walk in the counsel of the wicked,
or stand in the path of sinners,
or sit in the seat of scoffers!
But my delight is in the law of the Lord,
and in His law I meditate day and night.
I will be like a tree firmly planted by streams of water,
which yields its fruit in its season
and its leaf does not wither,
and in whatever I do prospers."

You can also insert your name into the scripture:
How blessed is (your name) who does not walk in the counsel of
the wicked... etc.

5. Sing the Scripture. Yes! Sing it! Just make it up. Singing opens
   our hearts as well as our minds and our spirits. (Besides, God
   loves to hear you!)

6. Memorize the verse or verses. You can print it off on an index
   card to carry around or in your phone. Walking, driving, washing
   dishes etc. are all good times to work on memorizing a powerful
   word from God. You may want to learn the verse by making a
   visual reminder. We can actually remember images easier and
   faster than words. Go to Morning Expressions at https://www.
   janecookcreate.com to see some ideas or actually do a Morning
   Expression with me there.

7. Paint it, draw it, and express it in any way while you meditate
   on it. The result may be very abstract. The point is to meditate
   on it while you create.

8. Express the scripture in movement and dance as you meditate.
   You might want to check out Praise Moves by Laurette Willis[1] at
   https://www.youtube.com/watch?v=jsxM8y4lfPs

ACTIVATION
REVERSE PRAYER

When you are feeling, thinking, and experiencing any of the nine obstacles which are in section III What's Stopping You? or any other negative thoughts concerning your dreams and desires for your life, reverse it by writing out the opposite as a prayer, claiming and receiving God's intervention to any negative thoughts.

Here is an example:
> Start with the scripture in II Corinthians 10:5 which tells us to
> "*...take every thought captive to the obedience of Christ.*"

"I take this thought that 'I don't know what I am doing. I don't think that I can do it,' captive and make it obedient to Christ who says that '*I can do all things through Christ who strengthens me.*' *Philippians 4:13.* I am learning. God, You have all wisdom, and You give wisdom to those who ask. God, I ask that You show me what I need to know. I am being led and guided to know clearly how to do the next step. I do not need to run ahead. I take action on what I see and know to do. The next step will open up to me when it is time. I am not alone in this process. God, You are with me every step of the way. You will never leave me. Thank you for your wisdom and understanding. Thank you for giving me wisdom. When I don't know, You do! You know how. I trust in You. You have good plans for me. Amen." (James 1:5, Proverbs 3:5-6, Deuteronomy 31:8, Isaiah 41:10, Jeremiah 29:11)

After you write your reverse prayer, pray it, and read it out loud to yourself. Select one affirmation that spoke to you the strongest. Write it on a card or slip of paper. Carry it with you. As you walk and go about your day, repeat it out loud and in your mind. You will reprogram/renew your thinking in this way.

#17 AS YOU EXPAND INTO YOUR CREATIVITY AND FULFILLING THE VISION, REALIZE EXPANSION REQUIRES STRETCHING. YOU WILL FEEL IT. KEEP GOING.

THE BOTTOM LINE for my work with the women in Cambodia was that we overcame. I went back to work four days after I got out of the hospital after the ruptured appendix. I was stretched. It was a challenge, but I climbed the five flights of stairs two times a day, laid down on the floor in front of the fan when I got tired, and the girls carried on. We got the artisan group started. We created beautiful handmade beads for unique jewelry in a short amount of time. We were able to have product for our first art show as "Nokor Creations," which means "Kingdom Creations" in Khmer. The queen's representative made an appearance at the art show. We were pleased that she stopped at our booth. She liked the name of our artisan group. We sold our very first pieces. We received feedback and encouragement to continue.

Keep Going
"Rather than waiting to be rescued from the hard journey,
Continue on.
Just as the rivers come together and merge into the sea,
The 'larger than'—So will you. Keep on!"
—jane

ACTIVATION
ENCOURAGE YOURSELF

Read some inspirational stories or listen to TED talks or pod casts of the power of ONE and how ONE person can make a difference and how people have overcome great difficulties.

Read back over your journal about your journey so far.

Look at the Vision Poster or your Vision Board Collage.

Speak scriptures, quotes, declarations, and affirmations over yourself that are meaningful to you.

Listen to your visualization of your dream that you recorded.

Watch an inspirational movie based on real life or not.

Create play lists of inspiring songs.

Examples:

Books: *The Butterfly Effect* or *The Noticer* by Andy Andrews, *Love has a Face* by Michele Perry, *Compelled by Love* by Heidi Baker, *Always Enough* by Heidi Baker, *The Invention of Wings* by Sue Monk Kidd, *The Pursuit of Happiness* by Chris Gardner, *On Fire* by John O'Leary

Movies–*The Boy Who Harnessed the Wind*, *Madam CJ Walker* (the 1st female millionaire), *The Secret Life of Walter Mitty* , *The Pursuit of Happiness*

Songs: "Fear is a Liar" by Zach Williams, "Nobody" by Casting Crowns, "The Breakup Song" by Francesca Battistelli

#18 BE WILLING AND PREPARED TO DO THE WORK. SEEING A VISION COME INTO BEING TAKES WORK AND WILL CONTINUE TO TAKE COMMITMENT AND WORK. IT IS A JOY, BUT IT IS ALSO WHERE THE "RUBBER MEETS THE ROAD." DO THE WORK.

I DID A quick turn-around trip back to Cambodia a few months later to keep nurturing and teaching the new artisans. Since we had already started, I returned with great expectations to teach and to take them farther on their artistic journey. That truly did happen. It was an amazing and beautiful time amidst the high temps and the power shut downs each day. But there was a new challenge. The vision needed to be defined, the mission stated and the roles and goals clearly expressed with everyone on the same page, and a business plan in place. All of this came to the surface on this trip, and much time was spent writing and rewriting it all out with much discussion and also pain as some on the team chose not to continue. Though it was a long process (we are still working on aspects of it), it is so very necessary for the success of the business. I had to realize that even in the bliss of seeing the vision coming to fruition, there is still much nitty-gritty work to be done. Don't be discouraged or judge yourself or your work too harshly. It could simply be too soon to tell. You may not even know the results of what you do. What you do may affect generations after you.

"Sometimes you have to plow under one thing
in order for something else to grow."
—Ernest J. Gainer

ACTIVATION
DO THE WORK

Schedule out your time for what you need to do to make progress.

Decide your intention for each day.

Schedule in your calendar and daily routine when you will work on certain
projects and the steps necessary to pursue the dream.

There are lots of ways to do this. A simple calendar works, but I have
found 2 other ways that help me to see progress.

I created a graph paper progress chart so that it has multiple projects and
routines on it with boxes that can be checked. I like it because it helps
me to see the big picture and also to track multiple projects or areas
of my life. I use graph paper because it is already divided up into the
little squares. I divide the space up into all the things that I want to
work on across the top of the page. I write the date down the left
margin. I make check marks into the correct space when I complete
it or length of time I worked on it etc. It makes it easy for me to take
a quick glance and see what I need to do and how I am doing overall.

I use it for personal and for work; body, soul, and spirit.

Another way to visually track your progress is a minimal journaling
technique I read about on Michal Korzonek's Medium Blog.[1] You
can pick whatever you want to include in the tracking. You can include
personal habits and goals as well as project goals. You could include
exercise, time in nature, what you eat – fruit, vegetables, meat etc.,
time you get up, time you go to bed, amount of productive time,
meditation, art, writing, quality of human interaction, days lived so
far, etc. You can set it up any way you wish. What you track is up to
you. It's a great way to have a quick overview.

Go to your free course to see an example of the graph and also the minimal
journaling technique.

#19 SOMETIMES ON THIS JOURNEY, THE VISION OR CREATIVE IDEA MAY TAKE AN UNEXPECTED TURN OR LOOK A LITTLE DIFFERENT THAN YOU EXPECTED. BE WILLING TO SHIFT.

YOUR DREAMS HAVE a life of their own. Let your dreams become different than what you first imagined. Let your dreams evolve as you move forward. Even after I got home, I continued to have more understanding of how the business could work and ideas continued to be shared. The final decision required me to shift again from what I had expected. That in itself can be difficult when your heart, soul, and investment has been 100%. Yet, as I took the time to get quiet and open about it, I got a new perspective and realized that the new plan would actually release me so that I would be available to pursue the even bigger vision I had had to help many groups of women artisans around the world!

Vision changes as you go. Your vision may develop and evolve differently than you first expected. Go with it. It is most likely headed for something even more inspiring. There is a bigger picture. I expected to work with maybe one group of artisan women, but due to different ideas and desires of people involved, I then saw an even bigger vision and am currently helping many different groups of women around the world. Shifts can be difficult. God's plans for you are even bigger than you could possibly hope, think, or imagine (Ephesians 3:20).

Don't over analyze or try to "cling" to your first vision when there is a flow. Take the steps as they come. Act on what you are seeing. Receive it, and do the next thing that you feel is in line with your dream. Keep moving. What you do triggers something you did not see before, and on it goes until the vision is realized. Matthew 7:7-8 reminds us to ask, to seek, to knock, and we will receive, find, and discover an open door. We ask, seek, and knock with intention, expectation, and gratitude. We are not anxious or fearful. Before we call, God is answering (Isaiah 65:24).

Don't stop your forward process by being too attached to your original ideas. Often when you take action and move toward your vision, there can be changes in direction. It can catch you off guard like it did me, but don't limit yourself. Take some time. Look at it from a different perspective. Be willing to realize there may be an even BIGGER plan than what you thought in the beginning. Be willing to change and to shift. Trust that God's plan and perspective is so much bigger. Trust Him to lead you. Then do the work! Remember it's the purpose that stays the same, and it's the purpose that motivates you to do the work. It matters. It can truly make a difference. It can change people.

When you are in the stream, you are a part of something powerful, yet you do not know exactly where you are going, but the stream will take you to an even bigger place of abundance, opportunity, provision, connection, and unity. There is a surrender and a trust when you are in the stream, in the flow of something more powerful than you, larger than you.

First, we accept who we are and how God has made us with our unique combination of gifts, passions, experiences, and skills. Then, we must be courageous enough to go after what is in our hearts to do. Finally, we realize that we are just a small part in a much bigger story. We are a part in an eternal story. In giving of ourselves, we connect to the larger story with purpose. We find joy in focusing less on ourselves and our small concerns by joining to the larger and grander plan of God's design, love, and connection.

ENCOURAGEMENT FOR YOUR JOURNEY

YOU HAVE HEARD a little part of my story. My whole desire is that YOU see that God wants to use "average, ordinary" people like me, like you, to impact the world with creativity and love. The really amazing thing is that as we do, we discover that we ARE actually extraordinary! We are choosing to act and live in faith. We make the impossible possible! We create. We make the invisible idea/vision visible! We are extraordinary not just because we are "doing" something, but we discover that we ARE truly unique and the world needs us to be ourselves. By shining, we give others permission to be themselves as well. We all are extraordinary, because we are all different. Maybe you feel too different? Or odd? I feel that way at times too. In 2015, I had a journaling experience when I was praying and God began to speak to my heart about this, and I wrote it down. I want you to insert yourself into this revelation because it is for you too!

> "You were not named Dorothy Jane/ (Your name)
> for no reason.
> Both names mean 'Gift from God.' (What does your name mean?)
> You truly are My gift to your parents, siblings, husband, children, grandchildren, friends, and to the world. You are not only 'tolerated' as the enemy would tell you. I give only good and perfect gifts. You are specifically designed to minister to those in your sphere of influence. You are strategically placed. I have given you the gifts, abilities, and passions for where you are. If you feel like an 'odd duck,' it's because I have placed **you** there to bring **you**, with all that **you** are, to that place, because without **you**, **you** would not be there, **your** light, **your** seasoning, **your** perspective, **your** work, **your** influences. So don't be looking for someone who understands you perfectly and thinks exactly like **you**. They won't be able to, but it does not mean that you **don't** belong. It means that **you** must be where **you** are or the expression of Myself through **you** will not be there if **you** do not just go ahead and release all that I have put in **you**! Don't look around you for confirmation, but move according to what is within **you**, My Spirit. And by the way, **you** are NOT too old (or too young) to accomplish ALL that I have planned for **you** ... You have no idea of the adventure ahead of **you**!"

So, what is in your hands? I had jewelry making, bead making, wire bending skills, and a heart to help women use their creativity to create sustainable income for themselves and their children, to create freedom from poverty and slavery, to create beauty and connection, to create a legacy to pass down to their children and future generations, to change their village, city, and nation for good. It can be just a small thing. Beads are small. But the effect can be huge! Seeds are also small and dry, yet when planted and watered, they grow and multiply!

There is a beautiful story that demonstrates this idea of how one person can impact the world in a huge way and how each one of us matters. We make a difference for better or for worse. I read this story in the *Butterfly Effect* by Andy Andrews.[1] The butterfly effect was a theory presented by Edward Lorenz in 1963 that a butterfly could flap its wings and set molecules of air in motion, which would move other molecules capable of starting a hurricane on the other side of the world. He was laughed at until 30 years later when the theory became a law known as the Law of Sensitive Dependence Upon Initial Conditions. This law of effect, or the first movement of any form of matter, includes people. He then proceeds to tell this story—the Butterfly Effect.

WHO drastically changed the world and saved 2 billion+ lives?

Was it Norman Borlaug? He hybridized high yield, disease resistant corn and wheat for arid climates. His seeds grew where no other seeds ever thrived before, and he therefore saved over two billion lives.

Or was it Henry Wallace? Henry was the Vice President under Franklin Roosevelt. He was the former Secretary of Agriculture who created a station in Mexico whose sole purpose was to hybridize corn and wheat for arid climates. Henry hired Norman Borlaug (who won the Nobel Prize) to run it.

Or was it George Washington Carver? George, as a university student, took the six-year-old son of his dairy science professor on "botanical expeditions." The boy absorbed George's love for plants and what they could do for mankind. George developed 266 things from the peanut and 88 things from the sweet potato AND spent time with six-year-old Henry Wallace.

Or was it Moses, a farmer in Diamond, Missouri? Moses didn't believe in slavery and suffered the consequences as Quantrill's Raiders burned his barn, shot several people, and drug off Mary Washington who refused to let go of her baby, George. Moses and his wife set up a meeting with the Quantrill's Raiders to trade his only horse for the baby. They met at a crossroad in Kansas, and threw him a cold, naked, barely alive baby boy in a dirty burlap bag. Moses held the baby inside his shirt and walked home that cold night. The baby lived. Moses and his wife took care of him, educated him in honor of his mother, Mary, and gave him their name, Carver. George Washington Carver.

So, WHO saved the 2 billion+ people?

Do you see the chain? We are also in chains of action for good or for bad. Our decisions, what we do every day, big or small, *all* make a difference today AND actually in the future, forever! Energy ripples on and causes shifts, and the ripples go on and on. There *is power* in ripples! Ripples are continuous and consistent. Even a smile changes the world. Everything you do ripples on forever and changes things, no matter how small you think the act is. And everything ripples back in reaction, sending it back to you, multiplied!

> *"Few will have the greatness to bend history, but each of us*
> *can work to change a small portion of events and in total of*
> *all those acts will be written the history of a generation ... It*
> *is from numberless diverse acts of courage and belief that*
> *human history is thus shaped. Each time a man stands up*

for an ideal, or acts to improve the lot of others, or strikes out
against injustice, he sends forth a tiny ripple of hope, and
crossing each other, form a million different centers of energy
and daring, those ripples build a current which can sweep
down the mightiest walls of oppression and resistance."
—*Robert Kennedy*

"Every great change starts like falling dominoes."
—*BJ Thornton*

Find the one thing that by doing it everything else will be easier. Find the first domino to start the chain. Each part of the chain is simply a small thing, a small step that contains potential energy. Once you start toward your vision, little by little and suddenly you will gain momentum to accomplish amazing things.

"There is not a person alive who is not capable of greatly
contributing to the well-being of this planet.
Just changing your attitude can affect
the world around you."
—*Susan Jeffers*

What actions have you taken and have seen the results of your action in a chain of events or a domino effect? Write it out now. Here is one of mine of the events leading up to going to Haiti after the earthquake.

"The moment one definitely commits oneself,
then Providence moves too.
All sorts of things occur to help one
that would never otherwise occurred.
Whole stream of events issue from the decision
when no one could have dreamed
would have come their way."
—W.H. Murray

I went with a medical team to Haiti after the 2011 earthquake. After working in the tent villages, we ended up at Port au Prince Hospital as doctors and nurses were in demand as some were having to return home. Since I had no medical qualifications, I worked in the supply tent and yard to try to organize the vast amount of supplies coming in from around the world. Besides the medical supplies, I found several tents. These became invaluable. When people were released, they had no home to go back to, therefore, the great need for tents. After I returned home, I just couldn't forget the devastation and need that I had seen. I let my customers at the Oasis Christian Bookstore and Coffee Shop know that I would be collecting tents to ship to Haiti. The response was a little disappointing. Then the newspaper and radio interviewed me and wrote an article. People responded.

One elderly man came in and asked about it. He had heard about the tent collection on the radio. He came back later with four big, expensive tents. He had spent at least $500. I went out to his car to help him carry them in. It was the oldest, rustiest car I'd seen in a long time. I got choked up and wept. The $500 was most likely a sacrifice for him, but he wanted to help "those poor people who had experienced such destruction." He had the heart. We ended up with 263 tents and 252 tarps! Wouldn't you love to hear the "chain" that those tents created as they arrived and helped various people and families?!

"There is a spiritual chain reaction that occurs
the moment we act on faith."
—Julia Cameron

"Everything you think and do is a cause set in motion
and will have an effect on your life."
—Tony Robbins

I watched the movie of a true story called, *The Boy Who Harnessed the Wind.*² It's about another chain created by ONE, just a boy named William Kamkwamba who lived in Africa. His family and village were in a drought. Things looked hopeless. He began to see a creative solution as he looked at the world around him. He observed how a little mechanism, a dynamo, on a bicycle caused a light to come on. Even when he was no longer allowed to go to school due to lack of money from the failure of the crops, he pursued anyway and won over the librarian to study secretly in the library.

He read everything he could on creating energy and windmills. When he had the clearer idea on how to make one, even his own father ridiculed him and forbade him to work on it and ordered the boy to work in the fields with him. His mother understood his creative mind and challenged the father to support him and to give him his bicycle. It took great humility and faith in his son to agree. The boy persevered and it worked. He not only saved his family's crops, he affected the village and many others as they began to use windmills for energy to pump water to their crops in times of drought. *One* boy's invention affected all of his country. ONE boy!

"If you want to change the world, start singing
when you're up to your neck in mud."
—Admiral Harry McRaven

Admiral Harry McRaven shared a Navy SEAL training story about the power of ONE.³

As part of their Navy SEAL training, the men had to spend 15 hours, through the night, in Mud Flats (freezing cold mud up to their necks), with howling wind, and constant pressure and chiding by the instructors to quit. The men could leave the mud if only five men would quit. Many were on the edge, moaning and chattering. But then *one* voice began to sing, then two, then three, then everyone was singing. If *one* could rise above the misery, then others could as well. Even though they were threatened and told to stop, they kept on singing and stayed neck deep in the freezing mud for the full 15 hours. The power of ONE person can change the world by giving people *hope*. We can too. I can. You can. We can make a difference!

ACTIVATION
WHAT CONNECTION CHAINS DO YOU HAVE?

> Think about things that have happened in the past or things that are happening now where you see "chains" of connections, "happenstance", "coincidence" or divine direction and unusual unexpected occurrences have happened toward a particular desire or event.

> As you take the time to go through the chain of events and how people, places, and things came together, give thanks.

> Be encouraged that in the current endeavor to see your dream come into reality,

> God is working on your behalf. Release and rest in that place of faith.

#20 EVERYTHING YOU DO MATTERS!

"Everything you do matters! Every move you make. Every action you take matters ... not just to you but also to your family, your business, and your hometown. Everything you do matters to all of us forever."
—Andy Andrews

YOU WILL DEFINITELY want to get the book *The Butterfly Effect* to read the other story Andrews shares on how one man set up a chain of action that continued through many generations until today, saving millions of lives. He ends with this amazing thought:

"How far forward would we need to go in your life to show the difference you make? Every single thing you do matters."
—Andy Andrews

"In all labor there is profit, but mere talk leads only to poverty."
—Proverb 14:23

I believe that. Everything we do matters, every decision we make, and every choice. Talk must cease and action must begin.

Admiral McRaven mentioned this incredible fact in his speech: The average American will meet 10,000 people in their lifetime. If every one of us changed the lives of just 10 people, and each one of those changed the lives of another 10 people, then in 5 generations or 125 years, you will have changed the lives of 800 million people.[1] So, what is stopping you from just going for it?

*"If you were meant to cure cancer or write a symphony or crack
cold fusion, and you didn't do it, you not only hurt yourself; you
hurt your children. You hurt me. You hurt the planet. You shame
the angels who watch over you, and you spite the Almighty who
created you and only you with your unique gifts, for the sole purpose
of nudging the human race one mm further along its path back
to God. Creative work is not a selfish act or a bid for attention on
the part of the actor. It's a gift to the world and every being in it.
Don't cheat us of your contribution. Give us what you've got."*
—Stephen Pressfield, War of Art

*"I am only one, but still I am one.
I cannot do everything, but still I can do something.
I will not refuse to do the something I can do."*
—Helen Keller

Take that small thing in your hand, that "five loaves and two fish" and give it to Jesus. He will multiply it. All He asks is that we give what we have to Him for others. It's not about what we don't have. It's about what we have. It is about taking action. It is in the action that provision is made. Not just enough, but MORE than enough! After 5000 men plus women and children were fed by the miracle of the five loaves and two fish multiplying, there were twelve baskets full left over! God is a God of abundance.

Believing that God is the giver of every good gift and a God of abundance is so crucial to see the world through the eyes of abundance rather than lack. I thought I believed this, but realize I am still growing in this area. Here is an entry I wrote in my journal in 2014:

*"I have realized that this lack or 'not enough' mentality has tried to
creep in on me, especially since I made the move to sell the store
and to follow my vision to help women in developing countries
and here with creativity. I have felt 'there is not enough time.'*

I have felt 'there is not enough money.' I have felt that maybe
'I am not enough.' 'My artwork is not good enough,' etc. This
scarcity thinking is a lie to cause me to be depressed and to
stop the work. It is a lie to keep me from enjoying the moment
and trusting that 'all things are working together for good.'"
—Romans 8:28

"And God is able to make ALL grace abound to you, so that
ALWAYS having ALL sufficiency in EVERYTHING,
you may have an ABUNDANCE for EVERY good deed…"
—2 Corinthians 9:8

There is no shortage to accomplish all that God has called me to do! There is no shortage of time, energy, resources, or connections. God has no shortage of what you need. God has no problems whatsoever.

Be faithful with the small thing that is in your hands, and He will give you more. I received an encouraging word from a friend in 2018. He said, "Surely as I called Moses to lead My people out of bondage, surely have I called you to draw women out of deep darkness… For as I did the miraculous through Moses, I will do through you. Even as I called Moses and asked him, 'What is in your hand? Cast it down and see what I will do with it.'"

He was referring to when God called Moses to go rescue His people from slavery in Egypt. Moses was to use his rod, upon God's command, to work miracles, which were the plagues in response to Pharaoh's disobedience to let God's people go free. He also used the rod to part the waters of the Red Sea to escape the Egyptians, and to bring forth water from a rock in the wilderness for the people.

I received greater understanding about "What is in your hand?" from Moses' rod. Moses' rod looked like a common rod, it was, but when filled with the Spirit, when given to God, it became powerful to overcome the enemy and to set captives free. The rod could do whatever God said or told him to do with it. So will my skills of jewelry/art, what I have in my hand, these simple, everyday skills and ideas. What is in my hand can do mighty things and show forth God's will, glory, and power to lead a host of women out of bondage and into the promised land, the Promises of God, a land of milk and honey, which speaks of abundant provision!

The rod, being a common object, fooled and surprised the enemy. Yes, it was just a common rod, but in God's hand, it became supernatural and a powerful weapon against the enemy and a powerful weapon for the Kingdom of God.

What is in YOUR hand? Yes, you may think you are common and ordinary. What you have in your hand may seem common and ordinary, but when you give it to God to use for others, expect to see astounding and miraculous things happen that are beyond your own abilities and resources!

I would like to share with you about the parable I referred to earlier. The Parable of the Talents found in Matthew 25:14-29 is the story of a man who entrusted his servants with his possessions as he left on a journey. He gave five talents (a sum of money) to one, two talents to another, and one talent to another according to their abilities. The first man traded and gained 5 more talents. The second man did the same and received two more talents. The last man buried his talent in the ground. When the master returned, he rewarded and said to the first and to the second man, "Well done, good and faithful servant. You were faithful with a few things, I will put you in charge of many things; enter into the joy of your master." The last man was afraid and hid the talent. "You wicked, lazy servant, take away the talent from him and give it to the one who has the ten talents," said the master.

Be faithful with what you HAVE! That is all you are accountable for. There is no ceiling to your success. It all depends on you. It doesn't matter

where you start, with how much or how little. It's about what you do
with what you have. Zechariah 4:8 encourages us "not to despise the day
of small beginnings." So, what do you have? What do you know? What
are your life experiences? What gives you the greatest joy? What breaks
your heart and gets your passion up? What is the dream/vision you have
kept hidden or are just beginning to recognize? You might just have a
curiosity or interest in something. Check it out. Follow it up. Take the
step. Revelation must be acted upon. Faithfulness requires *ACTION*.

> *"A farmer never plowed a field by turning it over in his mind."*
> —*An Irish Proverb*

We can think about stuff and know stuff, but until we take action, there
will be no fruit.

Ephesians 3:20 (TPT) is a powerful truth:

> *"Never doubt God's mighty power to work in you and
> accomplish all this. He will achieve infinitely more than
> your greatest request, your most unbelievable dream, and
> exceed your wildest imagination! He will outdo them all,
> for his miraculous power constantly energizes you."*

God WANTS you to accomplish all your purposes.
God WANTS you to be fully who you are created and designed to be.
God WANTS you to prosper in every way.

> *"Abundant food is in the fallow ground of the poor."*
> —*Proverbs 13:23*

In whatever area we have lack, we may consider ourselves "poor" in that area, but God is telling us that it is NOT about what we DON'T have but that we give what we DO have to Him. We use what we *have*. We all have "fallow ground," ground that is unused and unproductive. We *do* have something in our hands in which God says there IS abundance, *MORE* than we need, for more sowing! We have the ability to increase the harvest, our results.

My challenge to you is to take a first step, a step of action. I guarantee another action will be revealed to you as you go on your journey. As your perspective changes, you can see things differently than from where you were before. There are times in my process of discovery that I was to go to a specific place just so I would be in the right place at the right time to see another key revelation or connection or direction. It is kind of like in a movie where they are hunting for a treasure, and they must be on a certain island, in a certain location, to see the glint of an object through the rock formation as the sun sets. We don't always know the "why" of what we feel led to do in the process. The point is to keep on moving and working in that direction. It will become clearer as you go.

> *"We see from where we stand."*
> —*Haitian Proverb*

We get new perspective and new revelation from another step, another location.

> *"What you see and hear depends a good deal*
> *on where you are standing."*
> —*C.S. Lewis*

In *Why Jesus Crossed the Road*, Bruce Main[2] tells the story of a man named Ryan who placed himself in the center of an impoverished, broken community, and how he began to see differently, which touched his heart, which caused his mind to work and his hands and feet to follow and created change.

> *"The key to achieving success is recognizing*
> *the significance of every experience.*
> *Everything you do either helps or hurts you.*
> *Once you realize that every action has*
> *consequences—good or bad—You are one step*
> *closer to becoming unstoppable."*
> —*John Buckman, Chief of Volunteer Fire*
> *Department of German Township, IN*

ACTIVATION
EVERYTHING YOU DO MATTERS!

1. The smallest little things matter. Everything you do matters. Think of some small thing that was said to you or done for you that was meaningful, encouraging, and life changing. It was a small thing, but it was a big thing in your life.

    Write about it in your journal. What was the situation? Who said it or did it? What did they say or do? How did it make you feel? How did it affect you? What change did it cause or what action did you take because of it?

    If possible, call or write to the person to tell them and thank them. If it is not possible, thank God for them. Tell their family.

    Today, be present with those you come in contact with. Remember that small things matter. Remember that what you say and do can be a big thing in someone's life, positive or negative. Choose to take opportunities to influence others for good.

2. Do whatever small thing you can do today that relates to your dream. There are opportunities *TODAY* to do your dream where you are, with the people you are with. You can love and serve today. You do not have to wait for the whole big dream or vision to be in place to begin. Use whatever is in your hands today. God will multiply it as you share it.

#21 REMEMBER THAT IT TAKES ONLY ONE SMALL ACTION TO BEGIN THE "ACTION CHAIN."

"If you want to change the world, start off by making your bed..."
—*Admiral Harry McRaven*

A STEP, AN action, sets up a domino effect or a chain reaction. Just one action will trigger more action. That is when you gain momentum.

Make that first step simple and easy so that you will do it. Break it down to a simple, easy first step and keep going! Newton's 1st Law is that "an object at rest tends to stay at rest, and an object in motion tends to stay in motion." It's the natural tendency of objects to keep on doing what they're doing. All objects resist change in their motion. So, make it easy to start. Make it a routine. Once you start, you will gain momentum. James Clear says to do the same "pregame" every time so that your mind, when you do such and such, is triggered or kick started to "this is what I do before I do this habit," (i.e., I put on my tennis shoes before I exercise, or whatever rituals you establish).[1]

The inspiration will come in the work, as you work. The motivation comes in the work, as you work. I have seen this over and over again in my daily life, but also in my art. Sometimes I don't know what to make. I don't even feel motivated to do it. I just start. I go to the studio. I put on my work apron. If I am painting, I just pick some colors and smear them on the page. Then I pick some collage papers I like and add them. AS I work, I see what to do. It can be this way with any type of problem solving. Sometimes, most of the time, you don't just get the whole solution. You start, and it comes to you little by little. So, whatever your desire is, for example, to write, block out some time for each day, create a comfortable, inviting place to write with your favorite pen and paper. Then show up and write. It will come. It could start off simply 15 minutes a day. You'll get motivated and inspired as you commit each day to work toward your vision/dream.

Many successful people have discovered the secret of taking small steps. You may want to check out Darren Hardy's *The Compound Effect*.[2] The Compound Effect is about reaping huge results from small, smart choices.

Small, Smart Choices + Consistency + Time = Radical Difference

In Brian Tracy's book, *Focal Point*, he discusses how to improve any area of your life by 1000%. Whatever it is that you want to improve, increase it by 1/10 of 1% each workday. This will compound to 26% each year and will double each 2.9 years. In 10 years, you will have increased 1000%![3]

Every choice, every decision we make right now, takes us one step closer or one step farther away from our goal. It's like the Seek 'N Find game we played as kids. When seeking for something in the game, we would be given clues such as, "You're warm. No, you're cold. Now you're hot!" Keep going the right direction. It may seem slow at first, but as you gain momentum, your success will compound quickly. There is power in consistency.

Are you beginning to see a convergence happening in your life? Convergence is the "bringing together of different components so that the sum of the parts is greater in value than the separate individual pieces." Convergence also means to "come together and unite in interest or focus and purpose." This is another beautiful thing about how unique you are. All these experiences, background, culture, education, skills, talents, gifts, business/work, etc. come together as your vision/dream emerges. It will surprise you. I have been so amazed at how painting, polymer clay, wire work, website design, books, learning, teaching, art, science, missions, travel, business of the bookstore and coffee shop, full-time art work, marketing, computer skills, journaling, writing, poetry, mixed-media, workshops, conferences, and being a daughter, wife, mom, and mima are all coming together in what I am doing now.

"Life is a collection of unique gifts, passions, desires, and experiences that culminate in something that many have labeled 'convergence.' Convergence is the point at which you are catapulted into your most important efforts. This combination creates a platform for our most rewarding and important accomplishments."
—Dave Yarnes, Intro to the Three Circle Strategy

I wrote in my journal about convergence:
"The past is returning, circling back around
to meet up with the now and future.
All things seem to be converging,
Creating a new season
Strangely familiar but different.
God doesn't waste a thing.
It is all coming together in an
Exciting and powerful way.
Open my eyes, my mind to
See new POSSIBILITY!"
—jane

All of your experiences, interests, jobs, and connections are what make you unique. The world needs you. I challenge you to begin. Or if you have started, to continue. Keep Going. Chances are, the dream is actually much bigger and more than you can think or imagine. Be willing to open your mind up to even greater possibilities. There are creative solutions to all the problems of the world. I want to be a part of the solution. I know you do too. That is why you have taken the time to read this book.

It is time to face whatever reasons you have for not pursuing your dreams. It is time for you to discover the root issues, to overcome, and to move past these obstacles. I believe you CAN do it! I believe YOU can do it! I believe in you! GO FOR IT! Have you figured out what is stopping you?

ACTIVATION
CHAIN REACTION/DOMINO EFFECT

Determine what small action step you can take today toward your dream. One small action triggers another action and another, until it gains momentum. Complete a small action today. It will get you moving to accomplish greater things and it will become easier as you gain the power of momentum. Don't stop. Do some small step each day.

Make your bed. Wash the dishes. Complete any small task to help you get moving to complete an action toward your dream. Make your first step of the day easy. Make the first step to your goal easy. Ex. If you want to write a blog or a book. Set your daily time to write. Create a comfortable, inviting place to write. Gather your favorite tools–pen, paper, lap top, etc. Then set your timer for 15 minutes. That's all. Write for 15 minutes. Most likely once you get started you will want to write more.

Be consistent with whatever work you need to do toward your dream.
Make it easy to start. Do it consistently.
Plan this now. Write it in your journal.
Prepare so that you have everything you need when it is time to work.

WHAT IS STOPPING YOU?

1. WHAT IS STOPPING YOU? FEAR?

IS FEAR STOPPING you? There are many fears: fear of the unknown, fear of failure, fear of not knowing what to do, fear you are not enough, and fear of what others think. I can relate. This entry is from my journal in 2016:

"I will NOT be discouraged or misguided
by others' opinions or mindsets.
They do not know me or the call on my life.
They cannot judge it, therefore,
I do not receive their disapproval.
Only one who can see the complete picture
from beginning to the end can judge it.
Only God sees and knows the whole story.
I keep my eyes on You, Jesus,
my water-walking, storm-stopping, food-multiplying,
healer and deliverer, lover of my soul
and of the whole world!
I will not be afraid to think differently or
to be different as long as I am hearing Your voice
and following Your path."

"What other people think of you is none of your business."
—Benjamin Hardy

"Sustain my spirit. Give me gumption.
May I out-love my critics and
amaze my loved ones."
—jane

*"Those who danced looked quite insane to
those who couldn't hear the music!"*
—*Frederich Nietzsche*

*"Excellence is the result of caring more than others
think is wise, risking more than others think is safe;
dreaming more than others think is practical,
and expecting more than others think is possible."*
—*Ronnie Max Oldham*

No one said you wouldn't have some fear, just don't let it control you. Do it anyway! I've had people say to me before, "Aren't you afraid to travel by yourself? Or be in a foreign country?" etc. I always say, "I didn't say I never felt a little fear now and then, I just do it anyway!"

The only way to overcome fear is to face it and overcome it!

*"The way to have courage is to envision over and
over again a positive outcome.
And then choose faith over fear."*
—*Cat Bennett*

*"You cannot discover new oceans, unless you have
the courage to lose sight of the shore."*
—*Andre' Gide*

*"The fishermen know that the sea is dangerous and
the storm terrible, but they have never found these
dangers sufficient reason for remaining ashore."*
—*Vincent Van Gogh*

Fear actually attracts the very thing that you are afraid of. Fear paints a very realistic picture of really bad and negative stuff happening. Worry is a poor use of our imagination and energy. Worry is like prayer for bad things to happen. Fear paints lies. It's up to you to believe it or to choose otherwise. What do you believe? Interrupt these lies with truth. Interrupt patterns of fear and procrastination by doing something out of the ordinary. Choose to respond in a different way. Even respond in your body to interrupt the pattern and make it easier to get out of that fear pattern, and choose to believe truth. For example, do jumping jacks, take a walk, collage, dance, shout, sing, laugh, and speak truth. Stop the downward spiral pattern, and then take a positive step of action toward your dream/goal/intent. Take back your power to choose.

> *"Worry is a self-fulfilling prophecy."*
> —David Cameron Gikandi

What do you believe? What you really believe determines what you do. Change how you think. Renew your mind. The strength to do comes from your undivided decision. You have made up your mind. What you do comes from what you think. Change your mind, and your behavior will change. Your mind is a very powerful and creative force. It is always creating. It is a must to guard your thoughts and to take every thought captive to the obedience of Christ. We must train our minds what to think on. We can choose. Philippians 4:8 (NASB) encourages us what to think on.

> *"Finally, brethren, whatever is true, whatever is honorable, whatever is right, whatever is pure, whatever is lovely, whatever is of good repute, if there is any excellence and if anything worthy of praise, dwell on these things."*

Fear and love cannot both exist at the same time. Change your mind to think with God's mind. Release God's strength into all that you do and think. Use your imagination to see who you really are in Christ and to see His promises coming to fruition in your life. Keep your mind on God, and Satan has to flee. Keep seeing yourself succeeding and seeing your dream/vision coming to pass and all God's good plans for you.

"The steadfast of mind You will keep in perfect peace,
because he trusts in You."
—Isaiah 26:3

FEAR > FOCUSED ON THE DEVIL'S PLANS > IMAGINATION OF IT > EMOTIONS/FEEL IT > DEPRESSION AND ANXIETY

FAITH > FOCUSED ON GOD AND HIS GOOD PLANS > IMAGINATION OF IT > EMOTIONS/FEEL IT > JOY AND PEACE

"He who fears he will suffer, already suffers because he fears."
—Michel de Montaigne

Fear and doubt are enemies of your dreams/visions. Remove all fear and doubting thoughts. Never entertain them or give them a place or a home.

"What you are afraid to do is a clear indication
of the next thing you need to do."
—Ralph Waldo Emerson

"When once a decision is reached and execution
is the order for the day, dismiss absolutely all
responsibility and care about the outcome."
—Professor William James

"Never fear. Even in the cyclone there is a heart of calm.
Go and follow the dynamic call on your life to its fulfillment."
—jane

How can we overcome fear? What overcomes fear? Marianne Williamson, in *A Return to Love*, described fear as a "call to love."[1] We do what we do for others out of love. Where does this kind of love come from? "God is Love …" (I John 4:8). If God IS love, then only as we spend time in His Presence, receiving His love for us, can we be filled with love. When we are filled with God, we are filled with Love. He is over all, and there is no fear in Him. Love overcomes fear! Love eliminates fear. It's all about love. Nothing we do matters if we don't have love. Love is eternal. Love is unconditional.

> *"Let all that you do be done in love."*
> —*I Corinthians 16:14 NASB*

Love is absolutely essential and the most important thing in our dream, our vision, our journey. None of it will matter if we do not have love, and even when we don't see the vision coming into reality yet, if we love, we have succeeded. Love always wins.

The Excellence of Love

> *"If I speak with the tongues of men and of angels, but do not have love, I have become a noisy gong or a clanging cymbal. If I have the gift of prophecy, and know all mysteries and all knowledge; and if I have all faith, so as to remove mountains, but do not have love, I am nothing. And if I give all my possessions to feed the poor, and if I surrender my body to be burned, but do not have love, it profits me nothing. Love is patient, love is kind and is not jealous; love does not brag and is not arrogant, does not act unbecomingly; it does not seek its own, is not provoked, does not take into account a wrong suffered, does not rejoice in unrighteousness, but rejoices with the truth; bears all things, believes all things, hopes all things, endures all things. Love never fails; but if there are gifts of prophecy, they will be done away; if there are tongues, they will cease; if there is knowledge, it will be done away. For we know in part and we prophesy in part; but when*

the perfect comes, the partial will be done away. When I was a child, I used to speak like a child, think like a child, reason like a child; when I became a man, I did away with childish things. For now we see in a mirror dimly, but then face to face; now I know in part, but then I will know fully just as I also have been fully known. But now faith, hope, love, abide these three; but the greatest of these is love."
—*I Corinthians 13:1-13*

I love the movie *The Secret Life of Walter Mitty!*[2] It is all about a man that does not say or do what he really wants to do, instead he just daydreams what he would do or what he would say, until one day he begins to like a woman who works in the same company. He has trouble overcoming his fear to connect with her. Through a series of events, a famous photographer has sent a negative for him to prepare for the last issue of *Life* magazine, but it is not with the other negatives on the reel. The company is also undergoing some transitions, and the new boss is a bully to him. He has great pressure to find the negative.

Due to the beginning of a relationship with this woman (he has fallen head over heels for her), he takes some action in the real world to go find the photographer and get the negative. He actually overcomes his fear as he imagines that she is there encouraging him on. He flies to Greenland, jumps out of a helicopter, swims from a shark, and ends up on a fishing boat. He goes to Iceland, rents a car, rides a bicycle and then a skateboard, and outruns a volcano. He flies back home discouraged that he did not find the photographer. He is fired. He thinks the woman is back with her husband.

He later discovers the photographer had visited his mother and gains another clue of where the photographer is. He gathers up his courage and goes after the photographer to the Himalayas. He has an amazing adventure and discovers that he had had the negative in his possession all along. I won't ruin the rest of the story for you, it's just too good. You've got to see it! But anyway, the point is that the woman believed in him, his mother believed in him, and the photographer believed in him. He overcame his fears because of love. "Perfect love casts out fear."

Another movie, *Susie's Hope,*[3] based on the true story of Donna Lawrence, also illustrates love overcoming fear. Donna, a lover of dogs, is pregnant with their first child. She is bothered by the neglect and abuse she observes of a neighbor's dog. She feeds and waters the dog when the neighbor is gone. On one such occasion when she turns her back to the dog, the pit bull viciously attacks her.

Donna barely survives the attack, nearly loses her leg, loses her baby, and her ability to have any more children. She struggles with nightmares, anxiety, and stress. She comes upon an abandoned eight-week-old puppy in the park that was close to death due to being beaten and set on fire. The dog is near death. Donna cannot stand to see the puppy die from such abuse. She is filled with love for the dog and overcomes her fear. She raised funds to save the pit bull mix puppy and later adopts the dog, Susie, as her own.

I found this story fascinating that even after all that Donna had lost due to a dog, she conquered her fears and chose to love the puppy. Her passion for animals returned. The abuser was found and prosecuted and when the laws were too lenient, Donna and Susie worked to see changes made in the laws of North Carolina for stricter punishments for animal abusers. This striking story of love overcoming fear reveals how the passion in her was not extinguished by trial and affliction but amplified. Donna and Susie made a difference. They overcame.

True black is the absence of all light. Darkness is the complete absence of light. Darkness is blindness to light. Light is everywhere, but fear, judgment, and suffering can cause blindness. We see when we experience light, love, peace, joy, and forgiveness. There is no fear in love. Fear is a liar. Don't give evil power your life through fear. Submit to God, who is love and light, and darkness must flee.

> *"God has not given us a spirit of fear,*
> *but of power, love, and a sound mind."*
> *—2 Timothy 1:7 KJV*

> *"Without a vision the people perish,*
> *but without courage dreams die."*
> *—Rosa Parks*

Do not be afraid of the "unknown." The unknown has a lot of amazing opportunities, potential, and rewards waiting for you. Step into the unknown with expectation to find amazing treasures and adventures beyond what you imagined. If you find yourself in a state of fear or a temptation to fear, do not go forward in a confused or worried state. Calm down. Quiet yourself and find peace. Take every renegade negative thought captive. Shut the negative talk down immediately. Remember, worry is like praying for bad things to happen. Worry is visualization that concretes the horror show into our minds. When we speak our fears, we agree with fear's story and give our power for life into the hands of fear. Fear is a liar. Find yourself in God and receive His peace and His love. Choose to visualize the positive. See the mission or dream. See life, joy, and love, and fear must flee.

"There is no fear in love; but perfect love casts out fear…"
—I John 4:18 NASB

While in Cambodia on the third trip, there was some confusion that I had to deal with. I always bring a book to read, and the one I believed I was to bring on this trip was *On the High Road of Surrender* by Frances J. Roberts.[4] This little book spoke directly to me so many times over the length of the trip. At the time I was dealing with confusion, the book spoke to me not to waver from clear guidance and not to be swayed in times of confusion to leave the path, but to continue on in faith. I was encouraged to take the time to receive God's peace to continue on and persevere.

Beware of the negative domino effect that will occur when doubt and unbelief open a door that leads to a negative downward spiral.

Doubt enters in > you ignore God's Presence > then fail to trust in God's power > which causes you to be thrown onto your own resources > you become increasingly conscious of your own limitations > which increases your fear of failure > resulting in an atmosphere that prevents divine operation/supernatural power > resulting in relying upon on your own flesh > which causes you to fail.

Or will you choose to believe, which will lead to a positive upward spiral?

Believe God's word and His promises> receive and soak in God's Presence > your faith is enlarged and you trust in His power > which causes you to have faith that He has infinite resources for you > you become increasingly aware that with God all things are possible and there are no limitations > which increases your faith for success and victory > resulting in an atmosphere of expectation that invites divine intervention and the supernatural power of God > resulting in a greater release and trust in God to take care of the problem or care > causing you to be completely successful.

Faith opens the door for God to work and do even more than you could imagine! We must fasten our confidence on God. Keep our eyes on Him. Move in faith. God does not fail. God is with you. Give Him time and freedom to work. Release your cares to Him. You cannot fail if you do not quit.

> "So often the risk that leads to revelation and then courage is,
> at first, a very quiet threshold that we must dare to cross,
> through which life waits like a secret hidden in the open."
> —Mark Nepo, Exquisite Risk

> "Creativity is an act of faith. As artists (I add as 'creative
> people'), we are sourced in the Great Creator, meaning
> that our funding and strength and power is limitless."
> —Julia Cameron

ACTIVATION
FLIP IT

Write out what obstacle or fear or negative thought you have about the nine obstacles presented in the book. Write out anything and everything that comes to mind.

1. FEAR: I fear _____.

2. FAILURE: I am afraid I will fail at _____
    _____ because _____.

3. AGE: I think I am too old to _____
    because _____.

    I think I am too young to _____
    because _____.

4. NOT ENOUGH: I do not have enough _____
    to _____.

5. PROCRASTINATION: I procrastinate doing _____
    because _____.

6. LIFE: _____ is happening in
    my life right now so I cannot _____.

    Maybe when _____ happens I
    can _____.

7. DISCOURAGEMENT: I am discouraged because _____
    _____ and I cannot _____.

8. LACK OF RESULTS: I don't see results in _____

_____ because I don't see

_____ happening. (expectations)

9. OVERWHELM: I am overwhelmed by _____

_____ so I cannot _____.

After you have written out ALL your perceived obstacles and negative thoughts for each category, flip each one to the positive and add an affirmation.

Ex. I am too old to start this big project. It's too hard. What could I possibly accomplish at this age? I should have started sooner. It is too late for me.

To–I am just the right age for me to start this project. It is not too hard. I can do it. It is not too late for me. This is the right time for me. I am just the right age to follow my dream.

Speak these positive affirmations out loud. You may want to use these affirmations in other activations.

2. WHAT IS STOPPING YOU? FAILURE?

IS FAILURE STOPPING you?

> *"The greater danger for most of us lie not*
> *in setting our aim too high and falling short, but in*
> *setting our aim too low, and achieving our mark."*
> —Michelangelo Buonarotti

> *"People who never make mistakes,*
> *never make anything new."*
> —Albert Einstein

> *"A man of genius makes no mistakes.*
> *His errors are volitional and are the portals of discovery."*
> —James Joyce, Irish Novelist

> *"It's the NOT doing it, when you knew full well you had the*
> *opportunity, that hurts far more than any failure."*
> —Hugh MacLeod

There is no failure if you are learning. The only way to succeed is to be willing to fail. No one afraid to fail succeeds. Every successful person has failed many times, from scientists and inventors, to artists and sports athletes. You must not be defeated by failure. Failure is just an opportunity for course correction. If you are growing, learning, and dreaming you will fail. Learn and keep going!

> *"Even if he fails again and again*
> *to accomplish his purpose (as he necessarily must until*
> *weakness is overcome), the strength of character gained*

will be the measure of his true success, and this will form
a new starting-point for future power and triumph."
—James Allen, As a Man Thinketh

"The risk of loss has to be there. You cannot create
genius without having skin in the game."
—Jonathan Fields

Sometimes things are difficult, hard, and hurt. We must press through and keep going. Focus on what you can do and know to do. Focus on God by faith and His Word. You only fail when you stop, when you give up. Keep going!

"If one dream should fall and break into 1000 pieces,
never be afraid to pick one of those
pieces up and begin again."
—Flavia Weedn

"Failure is the opportunity to begin again
more intelligently."
—Henry Ford

"I never lose. I either win or I learn."
—Nelson Mandela

Failure is actually a learning process. We do not need to fear failure because it actually teaches us, which makes us stronger. Failure can be considered as a success for it is simply a step to greater success. Failure is a part of the process, the journey. Times of failure will test and build your character so that you can handle the next level of success. You want a wide and deep, solid foundation to build your life, your dream, and your vision on. The failure also brings greater clarity to your vision or purpose. Failure can open your mind to explore and discover even greater creative solutions than you originally thought of. The error can actually motivate you and inspire you to search and explore different ways and solutions and cause you to think even more divergently.

To succeed, we just need to keep producing the ideas and attempting to solve the problems. If we don't quit, we will eventually succeed. We don't need to be so obsessed with productivity to get more done in less time or necessarily with a particular outcome. As we are on the journey, there will be times we may feel "non-productive." No one likes to feel like a failure, but one big win, one big discovery, one big idea/solution to a problem is worth all the attempts (so called "failures"). All those attempts were part of discovering the solution.

We can make a choice of what path we want to take. We can totally change paths. We can focus on something completely different and do something different. No matter if we are succeeding or failing, we can change course and follow our hearts, but we must be willing to see with new eyes and welcome the idea of a new possibility.

"Give birth to yourself every day. Rewrite your life. Make it a do over. Wipe the slate clean every day. Start with a fresh canvas, and paint madly each day without worry, without fear."
—Regina Brett

"This is the moment of decision, when who you are and what you want meet."
—Jeff Goins, Real Artists Don't Starve

When you are at these crossroads, be sure to seize the moment to decide what it is you want to do, because these roads are different paths leading to different destinations. At these moments of decision, we cannot fear what others expect of us and allow that fear to keep us from pursuing. When you have clarity, you see the vision, the dream. GO FOR IT!

"Only those who risk going too far can possibly find out how far one can go."
—T.S. Eliot

When I was pursuing my artwork, I began with a small step to do a few art shows. As my jewelry became more in demand, I went part time in my teaching. I had time to make more art and do more shows. After a few years, I chose to do my artwork full time. Not everyone was positive. My mother-in-law, who was a teacher, said, "But what about your pension? Your retirement?" There were lots of "unknowns," but I answered that I wanted to pursue what was in my heart to do now, not wait until "retirement," and plan best I could financially. There are no guarantees a person will even live until retirement. Others just gave looks of surprise when learning of my "risky" change of occupation, but my husband and my close friends and family were supportive. I may have had the worst critic in my own head that I had to silence with determination and hard work to do it and succeed.

It is very important what we believe about ourselves. I was not sure how successful I would be as a full-time artist, but I knew it was in my heart to do. I believed that somehow I would find my way. I chose to believe. And I would encourage you to not put your belief in what you DON'T want (failure, fears, etc.), but put your belief in what you DO want. Your faith is powerful! Your faith will have results, and the fruit follows according to what you believe. Follow your own path. Be who you really are. You cannot fail when you are who you are meant to be. You can only fail if you are trying to be someone else. Be You!

"God didn't call us to be successful, just faithful."
—Mother Teresa

"Most great people have attained their greatest success
just one step beyond their greatest failure."
—Napoleon Hill

"A life spent making mistakes is not only more honorable,
but more useful than a life spent doing nothing."
—George Bernhard Shaw

"Every loss you've ever had is temporary,
every victory you've ever had is eternal."
—Bill Johnson

ACTIVATION
OPPOSITES

➤ You may want to make a poster of this or just write it in your journal.
➤ Write down the 9 obstacles mentioned in the book.
➤ Next to each one write its opposite, the positive.

FEAR ————> LOVE

FAILURE ————> LEARNING

PROCRASTINATION ————> ACTION, SMALL STEPS

AGE ————> ETERNAL

NO RESULTS ————> FAITH–OPENED EYES TO SEE
POSSIBILITIES

NOT ENOUGH ————> ABUNDANCE AVAILABLE

LIFE DIFFICULTIES ———> COURAGE + PERSEVERANCE

OVERWHELM ———> FOCUS ON GOD & HIS PROVISION

3. WHAT IS STOPPING YOU? AGE?

IS AGE STOPPING you?

Do you think that you are too old or too young? There are tons of examples of young people changing the world; people in their later years, and every age in between, are changing the world. Every age in our life has opportunity to change the world, to make a difference. Never let age keep you from going for what is in your heart. As long as you are alive, you have opportunity. Take it! I had to overcome wishing that I was younger when I started this mission. I asked myself, "Where would I be now if I had started this when I was younger? Can I really begin and get this going for real to prosper and be sustainable?" But then I realized that God KNOWS how old I am. It does not inhibit Him in the least. And if I had not had all the prior experiences, I would not be the same person I am today. It is foolishness to let your age limit you in any way. So, get going young people! Middle-aged people! Older people! Joseph was 30 years old when he was given authority next to only Pharaoh. Moses was 80 years old when he led the people out of Egypt. Abraham was 100 years old when he and Sarah had Isaac. Many, many people of all ages are doing what they are called to do. Go for your opportunities now. Today.

"Anyone who stops learning is old, whether 20 or 80."
—*Henry Ford*

Here are some examples of people accomplishing amazing things no matter their age:

40 yrs. – Hank Aaron hit his 715th home run.

44 yrs. – George Washington crossed the Delaware River and captured Trenton, NJ.

50 yrs. – Martha Stewart transformed her business into a lifestyle business. At 76 years, she has a show with Snoop Dogg, meal kit brand, 87 authored books, and a net worth estimate of $300 million.

51 yrs. – Julia Childs began her PBS cooking show, "The French Chef."

62 yrs. – JRR Tolkien published the first book of the "Lord of the Rings."

65 yrs. – Colonel Sanders started Kentucky Fried Chicken.

75 yrs. – Nelson Mandela was elected President of South Africa

76 yrs. – Grandma Moses (Anna Mary Robertson) started painting as she could not embroidery any longer. Three years later, her art hung at the Museum of Modern Art in NY. She wrote her memoir at 92 years old.

77 yrs. – John Glenn became the oldest person to travel in space. He rode the space shuttle Discovery nine days and orbited the earth 134 times.

94 yrs. – George Burns performed in Schenectady, NY, 63 years after his first performance there.[1]

"It's not the age, it's the vision...
Age is just a number."
—Arkenea.com

Ann Landers (Ann Landers was the pen name for Ruth Crowley and later Eppie Lederer, columnists who answered readers' questions and gave them advice. This column ran for 56 years from 1943 to 1999) is quoted as answering someone bemoaning their age because they felt they were too old to go back to school. Ann asked, "How old will you be in four years if you don't go back to school?"[2] Age is a moot point. I am proud of my mom for going to nursing school at 43 years old and pursuing her dream. I am proud of my sister for becoming a mom to two babies at 45 years old and pursuing her dream for children. Don't let age keep you from your dream. You are what you are today. Be you today. Do the steps for today. Each and every one of us, no matter how young or how old, can bless the world around us and contribute to its love and beauty.

> *"A zestful life of energy and vitality reaps*
> *longevity synchronized with God's rhythm*
> *and attitude for Life."*
> —jane

We love and adore the energy and enthusiasm of youth, but we must not forget or overlook the wisdom and depth that is established over time in the aged. We each have a place in this big beautiful world of infinite opportunity and possibilities! Let us encourage, support, and learn from one another.

> *"...men and women who refuse to stop growing, dreaming, and*
> *risking. In some ways, it's like a second childhood with all the*
> *benefits of the wisdom accumulated over time. You need both the*
> *wisdom and the wonder for your life to become a masterpiece."*
> —Erwin Raphael McManus, The Artisan Soul

> *"Creativity occurs in the moment,*
> *and in the moment we are timeless."*
> —Julia Cameron

4. WHAT IS STOPPING YOU? NOT ENOUGH? IS NOT ENOUGH STOPPING YOU?

DO YOU THINK that you are not enough? Do you think there is a scarcity? Lynne Twist addresses the scarcity mentality versus the abundance mentality in her book, *The Soul of Money.*[1] Her book deeply impacted me.

Lynne points out that in our world of abundance, we tend to focus on lack. She says, "For me, and for many of us, our first waking thought of the day is 'I didn't get enough sleep.' The next one is 'I don't have enough time.' Whether true or not, that thought of *not enough* occurs to us automatically… We spend most of the hours and the days of our lives hearing, explaining, complaining, or worrying about what we don't have enough of. We don't have enough time. We don't have enough rest. We don't have enough exercise. We don't have enough work. We don't have enough profits. We don't have enough power… We don't have enough weekends. Of course we don't have enough money—ever. We're not thin enough, we're not smart enough, we're not pretty enough or fit enough or educated or successful enough or rich enough, etc." I've always thought I was a positive person, but her book opened my eyes to see where these thoughts were sneaking in. If you have ever had these thoughts, like I have had, you may want to try a new lens to see the world through—a new lens of abundance, fulfillment, and satisfaction, instead of inadequacy, lack, and dissatisfaction.

I found my belief in abundance in what God's Word says in II Corinthians 9:8:

> *"And God is able to make all grace abound to you, so that always having all sufficiency in everything, you may have an abundance for every good deed."*

Treasure and use what you have, what is already there! Believing that there is ALWAYS enough inspires sharing, collaboration, and contribution. Believing involves releasing, knowing that no matter what the moment looks like right now that what you desire is in process. We must stay present in the gifts of *now* and appreciate what we have and use what we have!

Every moment, every hour, every day is full of possibility. You can choose to take any small positive step every hour if you desire. Time does not care about the past times that you did not do something. Time just generously continues to give you a fresh opportunity each moment. There is no advantage to wait until tomorrow when you have the present moment. The secret of success and productivity, I think, is what you do and who you are right now, in this moment. Live in this moment the way your heart desires for your body, soul, and spirit, and you will live the life of your dreams.

"How you live this moment is how you'll live your life."
—jane

Constraints can be used positively. There was an intense season of caring for some loved ones, which I was blessed and happy to do, but I struggled with having only a few hours here and there to do some creative work I needed/wanted to do. One morning during my quiet time, I had the revelation that many times constraints help artists and business people actually accomplish more. I realized that I just needed to change my perspective. Instead of crashing and feeling paralyzed and overwhelmed, I could be energized and motivated with the same few hours.

It is a choice. It is in the mind. Flip it! Do I let the past, the time I could not work, or the future, when I cannot work, destroy the current moment, the NOW I have?! Right *now,* this *present moment,* is in my possession. All we ever have is the present existing moment. So, if I choose the present moment to work, I will be productive. I will have success. It is my choice, and I can achieve an amazing amount of work in short amounts of time if I am focused and seize the moment.

> *"I cannot succeed with an all or nothing*
> *thinking—nothing always wins."*
> —*Kerri Richardson*

I personally like to work in big chunks of time, so what will I do if I don't have a big chunk of time? Most days, I don't. I have finally begun to realize that I must work in the time I have and be grateful for it. Since I do love to work with a chunk of time, I will plan to have that time. I have been known to pack up some art supplies and go to my favorite retreat camp at Selah Among the Hills. But I have learned and am still learning to work with the time that I have. Little bits of time add up if I work at it day after day!

> *"Time is too slow for those who wait,*
> *too swift for those who fear,*
> *too long for those who grieve,*
> *too short for those who rejoice,*
> *but for those who love, time is eternity."*
> —*Henry van Dyke*

It has also helped to eliminate huge goals that I cannot control and focus on the steps, the process of what I can do and can control. It has helped me to have a greater feeling of success and motivates me to keep going. I will see the vision/dream to reality!

I can choose to be grateful and excited to have the present moment, or I can choose to be frustrated that I couldn't work yesterday. Do I want to feel and absorb such toxicity? Do I want to even carry that frustration over from any one moment into the present and actually choose to give the now to negativity? And working with constraints actually can increase productivity. Constraints are not something to overcome, but are actually giving opportunity for success and productivity. Constraints can actually work in my favor, for my good, and can accelerate my work!

Prayer About Time
"Well, Lord, I realize that I DO have some time in my
days though not my 'ideal' or in my control,
but I CAN control what to do with the time I DO have!
It's not that I can't accomplish anything.
It's all in my mind and therefore, requires a shift in
attitude and energy to fill the moment I have
with these worthy pursuits, rather than crashing
emotionally and physically and giving into it,
rather than rising above and seizing the time,
though not my design or preferred schedule.
I need a mindset of, 'Wow! I've got an hour this morning!'
or 'I have all evening to create, write, etc.'
NOT focusing on what I don't have right now,
but focusing on what I do have.
So am I going to let these things steal from me
ALL my time?!
Or just the time needed and use the leftovers,
instead of moping that I don't have the time I want.
The time I have I need to enjoy and appreciate!"
—jane

To be present and to live in the moment is the key to everything. Don't beat yourself up over the past or worry about tomorrow. Stay focused on just this present moment—now!

Need a physical reminder?

> Slap your face and say, "Wake Up!" (Gently!)
> Say, "I live in the present moment, now!"
> Put your hands on your heart. Listen to your heart. What is your heart telling you to do and be right now in this present moment? Do it!

> *"It is said that the present is pregnant with the future."*
> *—Voltaire*

Do you feel that you are not enough? There is a convergence of skills, experiences, and passion in you that makes you unique. Do not compare yourself to someone else. You cannot be them, but they cannot be you either! Yes, they may be better than you in some area, but you are a unique combination. You may need to write down some things about yourself that you are good at or have done in the past and experiences you have had to see what a unique combination you are! Never believe you are not enough. Never compare yourself with another. You are the only you—no competition!

Do you feel you don't have enough? You do not need the complete provision to start. Just give what you have to one person or opportunity at a time. There will be increase as you give. Your provision will overflow as it is given out. Just like in the miracle of Jesus' feeding of the 5000 with five loaves and two fish, there were twelve baskets of food left! This principal is true not just for money, but time, strength, energy, connections, ideas, etc. God has given you the seed to sow. What is it? It is about what you *have*, not what you *don't have*. God has no shortage of whatever you need. He has no problem whatsoever.

"Abundant food is in the fallow ground of the poor..."
—*Proverbs 13:23 NASB*

There is abundance in what we have. If it is not seen, we are not working what we have. In whatever area in which you feel that you have lack, you may consider yourself poor in that area. This word says there is fallow ground. We have "fallow ground." We have ground that is unused and unproductive. It is fallow, just lying there waiting for action to be taken, waiting for us to dig and see what potential is there. There is great abundance in us and in our hands! We DO have something in our hands in which God says there is abundance, or MORE than we need, not just for ourselves but for others. We have the ability to increase our harvest by sowing more.

The point is to use what you *have*. Focus on what you really desire, not on what you don't have. Focus on what you really desire, not on the means to get it (not on money needed, etc.). Don't limit how it can come to you. Use the time you have, the energy you have, and the resources you have. You have enough. You are enough. If you give what you have, it will multiply as it is given and be more than enough to share.

Prayer of Enough

"God, I thank You for Your plans and purposes given to me. I delight to do Your will. I can do all things through You. That includes building the new farm home, making art, being a good MiMa, Mom, and wife, and creating the Empowered Women Create company. Nothing is too big, too hard, or too complicated for You. Your power in me is more than enough for all that I am called to be or to do. With You all things are possible! You are faithful, always! I just want to hear Your way, Your path, in Your time.

I have enough time. I have enough resources. I have enough understanding. I have enough money. I have enough connections. I have enough energy, love, and compassion. I am enough because You are in me working to finish the good work You started in me. Amen." —jane

"Never doubt God's mighty power to work in you and accomplish all this. He will achieve infinitely more than your greatest request, your most unbelievable dream, and exceed your wildest imagination! He will outdo them all, for his miraculous power constantly energizes you."
—Ephesians 3:20

God, as the Source and Creator of everything, never runs out of anything. When we are one with Him, our resources are unlimited. "We have an abundance for every good work!"

> *"Here's my point. A stingy sower will reap a meager harvest, but the one who sows from a generous spirit will reap an abundant harvest. Let giving flow from your heart, not from a sense of religious duty. Let it spring up freely from the joy of giving—all because God loves hilarious generosity! Yes, God is more than ready to overwhelm you with every form of grace, so that <u>you will have more than enough of everything—every moment and in every way. He will make you overflow with abundance in every good thing you do.</u> Just as the Scriptures say about the one who trusts in him: Because he has sown extravagantly and given to the poor, his kindness and generous deeds will never be forgotten. This generous God who supplies abundant seed for the farmer, which becomes bread for our meals, is even more extravagant toward you. First he supplies every need, plus more. Then he multiplies the seed as you sow it, so that the harvest of your generosity will grow. You will be abundantly enriched in every way as you give generously on every occasion, for when we take your gifts to those in need, it causes many to give thanks to God."* —II Corinthians 9:6-10

Prayer to Receive
"I turn my face to the Son
and receive what He has for me today—
All the assignments and opportunities
All the strength and joy and peace that I need.
I open my mouth, my mind, my heart, my arms.
I receive."
—jane

"Opportunities increase as they are taken."
—Sun TZU

"Know the true value of time; snatch, seize,
and enjoy every moment of it. No idleness.
No laziness. No procrastination.
Never put off until tomorrow what you can do today."
—Philip, Lord Chesterfield

ACTIVATION
WHERE DOES MY TIME GO?

Where *does* our time go?!! This is a great challenge to discover how we actually are using our time.

> I challenge you to write down exactly what you do all day for one week. Jot down what you are doing every half hour for 7 days. You will be able to see where you are using your time, and if you are using your time on what you value the most, or if you are wasting time on things that are not of importance to you. How you spend your time reveals what you value.

> Categorize your activities. Add up the time spent in each category. Compare how you actually used your time with what your priorities are.

> Select one area you would like to improve the focus and productivity on by increasing the amount of time. Commit to increasing the time spent in that one area, then increase each week until you feel that that area is solid. Then you can work on another area you want to improve on.

> Continue to keep a log to see your process. You could use graph paper to mark off your progress.

> Were you surprised by any of the number of hours spent in certain categories?

> Did you gain any insight into why you may not be progressing in any particular area or what time of day is your best work time?

5. WHAT IS STOPPING YOU? PROCRASTINATION?

IS PROCRASTINATION STOPPING you?

> *"Professional work habits prevent poverty from becoming your permanent business partner. And if you put off until tomorrow the work you could do today, tomorrow never seems to come."*
> —*Proverbs 24:33-34 TPT*

So true. Why? Because tomorrow will become today, and if you don't work today, you won't work tomorrow when it is today. Beware—perfectionism is a disguise for procrastination. Make work a daily habit, then you will prosper and have success in the thing you put your heart and your hand to.

> *"Every morning you have two choices:*
> *continue to sleep with your dreams*
> *or wake up and chase them."*
> —*Anonymous*

> *"There are seven days in a week and*
> *someday is not one of them."*
> —*Benny Lewis*

You don't need to wait to start. Start before you're ready. You never will be! Perfectionism or preparedness or knowing all the answers are all just forms of procrastination that tell you, "Not quite yet." Perfectionism paralyzes. What breaks this paralysis? There is only one thing—movement no matter how tiny. Just make any kind of movement today, and you are on your way. Do what you CAN do NOW! Just put it out there. You can always improve upon it later if you feel you need to. Your "lesser work" may actually be "amazing" to someone else! If you encourage even one person or help one person, is it worth it? Oh, yes! Especially if you are that one person!

We will always be on our journey of growing and learning. We will never feel totally prepared, but we must remember that we can only truly learn and move forward as we are working in the process. We are creative people. We will always have new ideas and revelations to explore, experience, and share with others. Let good be good enough for now and release the results to God. And honestly, God has more in mind for us than we could possibly do. Whenever He is involved, you will be uncomfortable. You will be stretched, because He is wanting you to learn to trust in Him and in His ability to work through you in amazing ways beyond yourself. For us it looks impossible, but with Him everything is possible!

Let's share what we have and keep going. We must focus on what we are able to do right now in the present rather than on what we might be able to do better in the future. Eliminate the "I'll do it later" and replace it with a simple small step of an action. Not a "knowing" but a being and a doing. Begin right now, today! The only day we have to begin is today, right now! When Alexander the Great was asked how he conquered the world, he replied, "By not delaying."

> "The road to someday leads to a town of nowhere."
> —Tony Robbins

What are you waiting for?! Take that first step NOW! You already know all you need to succeed. More information is not what you need. Action is what is needed.

> "If you wait for all the lights to turn green before starting your journey, you will never leave the driveway."
> —Zig Ziglar

Do not live in reaction to things, but choose how you want to spend your time. Be intentional. Do not let the "little foxes" come in and spoil the vine or steal the fruit you desire in your life.

"Catch the foxes for us, the little foxes that are ruining the vineyards,
while our vineyards are in blossom."
—*Song of Solomon 2:15*

What are the sly little foxes in your life? Time-wasters such as TV, Netflix, social media, games, etc.? Worries that you allow to take your energy and your focus? Or are the sly little foxes doing things that are good, but keep you busy with them instead of the things that take you closer to fulfilling your calling/dream? We can choose. Forget how you did or did not do yesterday. Don't worry that you can't do it tomorrow, just focus today, not later, but actually right now. What do you choose to do right now?

Chase those little foxes out of your vineyard. They are robbing you of the fruitful life you desire. Don't let life decide its pace for you. Make the choice. Busyness does not equal fruitfulness. Be intentional about what matters and joyfully, fully create and celebrate each moment. You will miss today, the present moment, if you live today based on yesterday. Each new day is an opportunity for a fresh start. Everything is in "flux." Everything is changing. Don't see today based on the way things were yesterday. Change your perspective, and release all that happened yesterday or what could happen tomorrow. Choose what you want today. Choose joy and love in this moment.

"Time is an illusion.
The only time that truly exists is NOW.
The distinction between past, present,
and future is only an illusion,
however persistent."
—*Albert Einstein*

You must make time for a daily routine of quiet and reflection. Make time to reset. Reflect on what is and is not working in your life. Assess where you need to focus your energy to live the life you desire. Take action in this area to make space and opportunity to do so. For example, maybe you need a vacation, a break, a rest. You can just keep on going and constantly tell yourself you need a vacation. Your body is crying out. Your mind is telling you. Your soul is emotionally thin. But until you actually sit down and mark out the days for vacation on the calendar, make the reservations, pack your bag, and go, it will not happen.

One year my "One Word" for the year was "action," so I made a mixed-media visual collage about action. I put the visual on my computer wallpaper screen. I put it on my phone wallpaper. I put a reminder on my phone to repeat daily at a set time, "Are you taking action?"

> *"Procrastination is the grave*
> *in which opportunity is buried."*
> —Jason Fried, Rework

We are free to choose. We can always choose our attitude and perspective for every situation.

> *"A good life is lived, not dreamed."*
> —Jonathan Fields, "Good Life Project"

The dream must move into reality where we live it. In 2010, I went to a conference in Pasadena, CA. In between sessions, I wandered the surrounding gardens. It was warm, and I purchased a drink that I was not familiar with. It was "Activate" vitamin water. I drank several and was surprised that they tasted just like plain water. I thought that was just how they tasted and trusted I was getting the vitamins, until one afternoon I read the bottle, which said that the vitamins lose their potency sitting in water so they kept them separated for maximum freshness and potency. Activate—it was hidden in the lid! I twisted the top part of the lid off and out came the vitamins into the water. Wow! What a difference in the drink. It was no longer plain water. It was tasty and powerful! Activation in our life needs the "secret ingredient" as well. We are activated when we are filled by the Holy Spirit. Jesus gives us the supernatural water of life, which is the Holy Spirit.

> *"Now on the last day, the great day of the feast, Jesus stood and cried out, saying, 'If anyone is thirsty, let him come to Me and drink. He who believes in Me, as the Scripture said, "From his innermost being will flow rivers of living water."' But this He spoke of the Spirit, whom those who believed in Him were to receive; for the Spirit was not yet given, because Jesus was not yet glorified."*
> *—John 7:37-39 NASB*

The Holy Spirit adds the freshness of God's revelation, experience, presence, and power! Release of the Holy Spirit is "hidden." We must seek and tap into the "secret." It is hidden that we might find it, not hidden to keep Holy Spirit from us.

> *"I will give you the treasures of darkness*
> *And hidden wealth of secret places,*
> *So that you may know that it is I,*
> *The Lord, the God of Israel, who calls you by your name."*
> *—Isaiah 45:3*

We are encouraged to ask.

> *"Ask, and it will be given to you; seek, and you will find; knock, and it will be opened to you. For everyone who asks receives, and he who seeks finds, and to him who knocks it will be opened. Or what man is there among you who, when his son asks for a loaf, will give him a stone? Or if he asks for a fish, he will not give him a snake, will he? If you then, being evil, know how to give good gifts to your children, how much more will your Father who is in heaven give what is good to those who ask Him!"*
> —Matthew 7:7-11

Seek God. Seek His Presence, Holy Spirit. Be continually filled and empowered by the Holy Spirit, not just a one-time thing, but continually for fresh revelation and power for each day and each situation. It is amazing to be reborn spiritually to life and to follow Jesus for salvation, but we must also be empowered by the Holy Spirit to tap into God's strength and power beyond our own. Holy Spirit is the supernatural God-part of activation. Yes, we take the steps, but He empowers us. It is the natural plus the supernatural.

The opposite of activation or diligence is to be sluggish, slothful, slow to duty, hesitant, inactive, stagnant, lacking energy, slow to respond, idle, or procrastinating. Wow... I really don't like any of those words. I struggle with procrastination at times. I don't want to let the opportunity of today pass me by or assume that I will be able to do it tomorrow. I want to be activated and diligent to live the life I desire to live. A sluggard thinks about what he wants to do or get but never takes action to make hopes reality!

I have to beware of making "soft choices" in daily decisions or choosing "ease," as it can become a way of life resulting in frustration. "Knowing" about something is not the same as *doing* it. You can only get that knowledge from your head to your heart by action, by doing it. All fruitfulness grows out of intimacy with God. Fruit comes as we abide in Him (John 15). When we don't know exactly what to do in a situation or how to move ahead, we can always love. Love is the main thing. Love is the main action. Listen to Holy Spirit for direction and revelation, then respond and move into that invitation with steps of faith. Holy Spirit will empower you to do it and provide an abundance for every good work. When we are faithful with the small things, we will be entrusted with more.

> *"Then he said to me, 'This is the word of the Lord to Zerubbabel saying, "Not by might nor by power, but by My Spirit,"' says the Lord of hosts. 'What are you, O great mountain? Before Zerubbabel you will become a plain; and he will bring forth the top stone with shouts of "Grace, grace to it!"'*
>
> *Also the word of the Lord came to me, saying, 'The hands of Zerubbabel have laid the foundation of this house, and his hands will finish it. Then you will know that the Lord of hosts has sent me to you. For who has despised the day of small things? But these seven will be glad when they see the plumb line in the hand of Zerubbabel—these are the eyes of the Lord which range to and fro throughout the earth.'"*
> *—Zechariah 4:6-10*

Holy Spirit gives us power. Revelation when we receive it, is actually an invitation to step into it. Do it. Don't just accumulate knowledge. What good is knowledge/revelation if it does not spur us to action? The revelation is actually evidence that God is encouraging you to do it and is showing you the way.

II Corinthians 9:10 teaches us that it is in the sowing that He multiplies the seed. It is in the action, the doing. You don't need the resources, the energy, and the time if you are just sitting on the couch. But you need it when you are feeding the hungry, drilling wells for the thirsty, loving the lonely, teaching the unlearned, etc. Abundance starts with giving what you have, then you will see a replenishment. Miracles are seen in the sowing. You will have more than enough!

"Don't wait for extraordinary opportunities. Seize common occasions and make them great. Weak men wait for opportunities; Great men make them."
—Orison Swett Marden

William Borden was such a person. He came from a wealthy family and traveled around the world with money from his high school graduation gift. As he traveled around the world, he experienced a growing burden for the world's hurting people, and he responded by deciding to become a missionary. It is said that he wrote two words in the back of his Bible: "No reserves." He began Yale University with a heart fully surrendered to Jesus Christ. His friends found strength in him. He began a morning prayer group and began outreach ministry to the widows, orphans, disabled, and drunks on the street. He also became interested in the Muslim Kansu people in China.

Even though he was a millionaire, and he was offered high paying jobs, William continued to pursue missions. He wrote two more words in his Bible: "No retreats." After graduate work at Princeton, he headed for China, but stopped in Egypt to study Arabic. While he was in Egypt, he got spinal meningitis and died within the month at 25 years old. Prior to his death, he had written in the back of his Bible two more words: "No regrets." His will distributed nearly everything to mission groups. William responded to his heart and followed his dream to help hurting people. He did this even in death.[1]

Don't let regret over past mistakes stop you. Forgive yourself and others. It's time. Move on. You can choose what you do today!

ACTIVATION
ACTION STEPS

If you have not written out the steps you need to take to see your dreams fulfilled, now is the time! Do it. It's good to write out a general overall plan, but what will get you moving are the *next* small steps that you will take *today* and tomorrow and the next. Get the momentum going!

ACTIVATION
DISTRACTION FAST

Sometimes when we are stuck and having difficulty moving forward, we need to fast. I'm not talking about food, but distractions. Sometimes we have so much noise in our heads from conversations, radio, TV, social media, and even reading, that we need to fast so that we can have inner silence and quiet space to connect with ourselves. Reading can be inspiring, but if there is too much, you can find yourself filling your mind with other people's words, thoughts, and ideas at the sacrifice of having your own. Commit to at least one week of fasting from these distractions. You can make a list of things you want to do if you like, but what you will discover is that after you get work done, you will begin to connect with yourself and your thoughts and ideas. You will get creative and play. You will break through the "stuck" you were in, into creative flow which will transfer to your productivity toward your dream. Record in your journal what you gave up, how you felt at first, what you did, and the result.

6. WHAT IS STOPPING YOU? LIFE?

IS LIFE STOPPING you?

Do you have frustration of not being able to completely focus on the vision? Do unexpected situations occur that seem to become obstacles to accomplishing your mission? Yes, stuff happens. Every time I have come home from overseas, things have happened at home unexpectedly that have required my time, my energy, and my love. After this last trip to Cambodia, I was home less than a week when my 95-year-old friend, with whom I have cared for for many years, had a heart attack. She survived but did not recover her ability to walk and had to go into a care facility.

Right after this time, my mother-in-law had physical issues and needed me to stay with her. She ended up in the hospital, rehab, and back in the hospital. She passed away a couple weeks later after living fully every breath she had. There are many more details, but you get the idea. We are all busy. We have spouses and children and grandchildren. We have work. We have problems and situations that come up. We go through difficult times in life that require our attention, energy, and love. During these times, it is important to remember and realize that when we love, we are doing the most important thing!

"I feel that there is nothing more truly
artistic than to love people."
—Vincent van Gogh

Demands and Expectations ... Life
"Yes, you have dreams and visions to pursue.
Yes, it requires focus, time, and diligence.
But how do you handle the Demands and
Expectations ... These pull you off course and
require your energy and focus.
These rearrange your schedule until you have no routine.
What do you do in these times?
Times of stretching, patience, and exhaustion?
I have to believe that that is when you are carried.
You keep looking up and know God is there,
Working in you, working through you,
Creating beautiful works of love.
You are just taking the 'scenic route.'
You will return to 'the Path' and enjoy normal,
routine days again with time to focus on the 'Big Dream,'
But today, I will enjoy and be present on
The 'path off the path.'
Join me?"
—jane

The most important thing we can do with our lives is to love. Be not dismayed. Love and move forward even in small steps as you can. Live in your present moment and not in frustration. Live in love.

"When Love comes knocking,
a precious sacred moment,
will I open the door or hang out a
'too busy—do not disturb' sign?"
—jane

There will be difficulties to overcome, but we always have choices; even if it is only a choice of attitude. People wonder when things are hard ... "Why, God?" "Where's God?" We will all face challenges.

Even Jesus' arrival into the world was not an "easy" one or in the manner we might have expected.

Consider these difficulties:

1. Jesus, God, came as a vulnerable baby to a typical family, and he had to grow up and go through all the human limitations and experiences.
2. Mary had to travel by donkey when very pregnant. Not comfortable or seemingly "timely" for her. Yet it was prophesied that the Messiah would be born in Bethlehem; there was a bigger picture than her personal comfort.
3. There wasn't any room left in the inns for them to stay. They were provided a stable—not fancy, not necessarily comfortable or where you would expect the "King of Kings" to be born.
4. It was not a friendly or welcoming political atmosphere. The King wanted this child killed. It was violent, and many deaths were caused as he sought to kill the baby Jesus.
5. Joseph had to leave their country and go to Egypt due to King Herod's search to kill Jesus. They did not know when they would or could return home when they left. They did not return to their home until after Herod died.

All these details fulfilled prophecy, but God could have made it whatever He wanted… So, it is curious He did not plan or choose an "easy" entry for Jesus, His Son. He did not "exempt" Himself from hardship. He chose it. It must be necessary.

Although it was difficult, there was also provision:

1. Jesus came in the flesh so He knows our weaknesses.
2. Mary made it to Bethlehem to give birth to Jesus.
3. They did have shelter. They had some privacy but were also accessible for the shepherds to come.
4. Joseph was warned by an angel of the political/government danger and Jesus was protected.
5. They were given direction at the right time.

So—If God allows us to go through trials and hard things, we can be sure that:

1. God understands since He came in the flesh.
2. We too can make it to our destination and give birth to His plans/purposes for us at the right time and place even amidst unwelcoming and even violent conditions.
3. We will have provision. He will take care of us.
4. He will warn us and protect us from the evil one to be sure that His perfect plan is accomplished.
5. He will direct us in times of uncertainty, when we cannot see or know the details of the whole plan.

Our part:

1. Be willing to submit to God's plan. As Mary said, "May it be done to me according to your word," when she was told she would give birth to the Messiah (Luke 1:38 NASB).
2. Persevere, go to "Bethlehem" or wherever our calling/dream is, do what is required.
3. Trust that God will provide for our needs.
4. Listen. Believe. Obey as Joseph did. When we hear from God, obey even if we don't know or understand all the details.
5. Trust when we receive further direction. Be willing to obey when given a new direction.

Vision gives us focused energy that empowers us to say "No" to certain things and "Yes" to others. It also gives us the courage to endure difficulties in the path of our destiny. There is provision in the process of becoming perfect, complete, lacking in nothing. There is provision, protection, and direction during the hard times.

Difficulties > Opportunities + Stirs up Power to Endure > Perfect, Complete, Lacking in Nothing

Trials and Temptations

"Consider it all joy, my brethren, when you encounter various trials, knowing that the testing of your faith produces endurance. And let endurance have its perfect result, so that you may be perfect (mature) and complete, lacking in nothing. But if any of you lacks wisdom, let him ask of God, who gives to all generously and without reproach, and it will be given to him. But he must ask in faith without any doubting, for the one who doubts is like the surf of the sea, driven and tossed by the wind."
—James 1:2-6 NASB

"My fellow believers, when it seems as though you are facing nothing but difficulties see it as an invaluable opportunity to experience the greatest joy that you can! For you know that when your faith is tested it stirs up power within you to endure all things. And then as your endurance grows even stronger it will release perfection into every part of your being until there is nothing missing and nothing lacking. And if anyone longs to be wise, ask God for wisdom and He will give it! He won't see your lack of wisdom as an opportunity to scold you over your failures but He will overwhelm your failures with His generous grace. Just make sure you ask empowered by confident faith without doubting that you will receive. For the ambivalent person believes one minute and doubts the next. Being undecided makes you become like the rough seas driven and tossed by the wind. You're up one minute and tossed down the next."
—James 1:2-6 TPT

"Quitting is a permanent solution
to a temporary problem."
—Zig Ziglar

"Getting over a painful experience is much like
crossing monkey bars. You have to let go at
some point in order to move forward."
—Anonymous

Life
"Though struggling through change,
Our heart is scoured and
Comes forth clean
with fresh perspective and wisdom.
We are transformed."
—*jane*

I have a journal that is just to express "rantings and ramblings." I think journals are for rantings, ramblings, reflections, and revelations, but I like to keep the journal I or others may read positive, insightful, and encouraging, so I like to have another journal to just get "stuff" out of my head. I have recently started collaging and painting over those pages. I love it! Some of the writing may be visible, but it is not readable. It's like getting something off your mind, then covering it over with beauty and letting it go.

ACTIVATION
WHY NOT?

➤ Pretend someone is telling you to stop pursuing your dream.

➤ What would you say?

➤ Why can you NOT stop until you have realized your dream?

➤ Why is stopping or quitting not an option for you?

➤ Write down what you would say.

7. WHAT IS STOPPING YOU? DISCOURAGEMENT?

IS DISCOURAGEMENT STOPPING you?

On this journey of discovering who we are and what we are designed to do, our creative calling, we will face difficulties. But difficulties give the opportunity for our depth of character to grow and develop. Difficulties and trials are to stretch us and to teach us to press into God and the strength and wisdom He has. Difficulties give opportunity and stir up power in us to endure and overcome. Difficulties grow us into the people we need to be for the next part of the journey.

When you are feeling discouraged, access anchors that help energize you and give you comfort and hope. These may be daily routines such as walking or time with God, music, memories from when we experienced success and empowerment, breathing, visualization of giving the problem or concern to God, positive quotes, affirmations, and scriptures, an action that is symbolic of brushing off the negative thoughts or crushing them with a dance of joy.

When you are feeling discouraged and feel like giving up, you may need to talk to someone you admire and listen to their counsel for you. You may want to have an imaginary counsel, a "Think Tank" of people you respect living or not. I ran across an interesting story in Dale Carnegie's book, *Public Speaking*.[1] It was about Theodore Roosevelt. There was an excellent picture of Abraham Lincoln in President Theodore Roosevelt's office. President Roosevelt said, "Often when I had some matter to decide, something involved and difficult to dispose of, something where there were conflicting rights and interests, I would look up at Lincoln, try to imagine him in my place, and try to figure out what he would do in the same circumstances. It may sound odd to you, but frankly, it seemed to make my trouble easier of solution." After your "Think Tank," be sure to write down what they say.

There may also be a delay between receiving the vision and it actually happening. How will you navigate that "wait time?" Will you lose faith that you are truly to do it or can do it? Will you become "discouraged," lose courage? Will you forget about it? Will you live a life of frustration? I was over 50 years old before I had the opportunity to go on my first mission trip (2009) and to begin to see any movement toward helping women. Yet all the years before prepared me for the right time. Even after the vision grew clearer and closer, there was still timing involved.

After I sold the store in 2014 and was in Africa for three months, a group of volunteers came to Africa to help. During a prayer time together, a woman came up to me and told me that she saw me with a building, a place for prostitutes and the broken to come, not to live there, but a safe place, a refuge to come to. The vision did not really make sense at that time as I had just sold the store, so I just wrote it down in my journal and wondered about it. It was in 2018 that I first went to Cambodia and began the Artisan group to help women have a safe place to work and create sustainable income. I am still on the journey. I walk on in faith and trust and take the opportunities and steps before me as they open up.

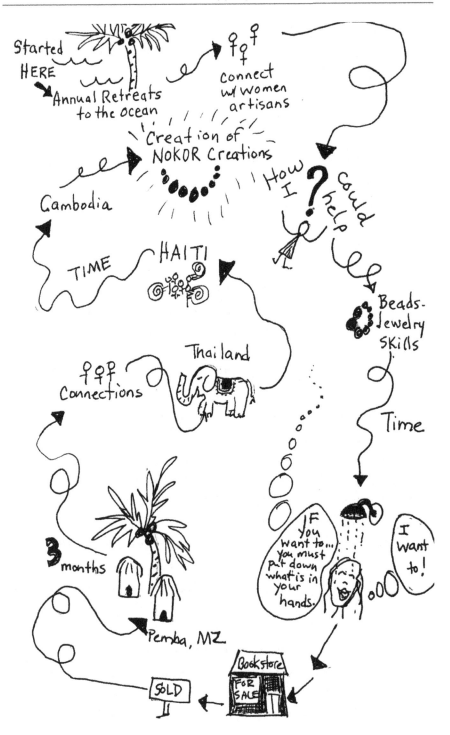

I am inspired by the life of Joseph and his example of perseverance through difficulties even when there was a very long delay of his vision/dream coming to pass.

Here's an outline of how it went down for him:

1. He was a favored son of his father. At 17 years old, he had a dream that was symbolic. He did not fully understand it. The family didn't like it, especially his jealous brothers. (You can read more details of this story in Genesis 37.)

2. Instead of the dream coming true, it looked like just the opposite was happening. His brothers sold him into slavery, and he was taken to Egypt to serve Potiphar. Negative feelings of self-pity, anger, bitterness, and unforgiveness could have developed. Joseph went from a "favored" child to a servant, yet he *chose* to work as unto the Lord. He maintained his integrity and was made overseer of Potiphar's house and all he owned. Joseph rose to a higher position, and Potiphar was blessed because of Joseph.

3. Joseph was faced with a difficult temptation, a choice to obey God and to keep his integrity or to succumb to the demands of Potiphar's wife. When he refused to have sex with her, she cried, "Rape." Joseph *chose* to do what was right, and he was wrongly imprisoned. He could have allowed feelings of self-pity, bitterness, anger at God, desire for revenge for being treated unjustly, depression, and indifference toward those around him to take over. But Joseph *chose* to continue to be a man of integrity and to rise above his situation. He was recognized by the chief jailer and was given a position over all the prisoners. Even in prison, Joseph overcame.

4. Joseph was 28 years old when Pharaoh's cupbearer and baker ended up in prison. They each had dreams they asked Joseph to interpret. Joseph looked to God for the interpretation and gave it to each one with a request to mention to Pharaoh of his plight.

5. Joseph remained in prison for two more years. Once again, he had the choice to be angry at them for not helping him to get out of prison. He could have become depressed. Joseph *chose* to persevere. He waited.

> *"Yet I totally trust you to rescue me one more time, so that I can see*
> *once again how good you are while I'm still alive! Here's what I've*
> *learned through it all: Don't give up; don't be impatient;*
> *be entwined as one with the Lord. Be brave and courageous,*
> *and never lose hope. Yes, keep on waiting—*
> *for he will never disappoint you!"*
> —Psalm 27:13-14 TPT

6. When Pharaoh has a dream, the cupbearer remembers that Joseph interpreted his dream and tells Pharaoh. This was in God's perfect timing for Joseph and for the good of others. His dream was about to come into reality. Joseph was called. He could have been too afraid and shrunk back or refused to go before Pharaoh to interpret the dream. But Joseph *chose* to respond, to have the courage to stand before powerful Pharaoh, confident in God. He may have felt inadequate and asked, "Who am I?" He may have thought, "I am not enough ..." Genesis 41:16 records that he put his trust in God to give what Pharaoh needed to know. Joseph was given the revelation and interpretation of the dream AND the wisdom and action that needed to be taken. The land of Egypt was to have seven years of abundance followed by seven years of drought. Joseph was put in charge of putting his plan into action. He was second only to Pharaoh. All of Egypt and the surrounding area's lives were in his hands, including his family.

7. Joseph was 39 years old when his brothers, who sold him into slavery and lied to his father that he had been killed by a lion, came to him to buy food in Egypt. They bowed down before him, just like in the dream he had when he was young, 22 years before. They did not recognize him. Joseph had the opportunity

for arrogance, pride, and revenge, but he *chose* to recognize God's hand in all of his life for a greater cause. His call, his dream, and his purpose was to save his family and nation and the lives of many others. He recognized that God was the one in control of his life, not his brothers, Potiphar, Potiphar's wife, or Pharaoh.

People may not always treat us right. The vision/dream may seem far, far away and be delayed. We may meet unexpected turns in the road, difficulties, and trials, but God has timing for us. God uses all things for our good, not just for us, but for others.

> *"...My times are in Your hand."*
> *—Psalm 31:15 NASB*

God knew the plans He had for Joseph. He gave Joseph a dream, which gave him hope.

Joseph persevered, and his trials strengthened and empowered him for his calling. God knows the plans He has for us. God gives us the dream to give us hope to persevere through trials. Focus on your dream/goal, but do not worry "how" they will be fulfilled or when you may think you need to raise money for your project, when God may want to give you the actual thing that you need, not the money. We will do better if we pray for what we desire. There are many other ways for God to give you what you need for the dream. Don't limit Him. Don't make deadlines for yourself, which create stress, fear, and doubt. Your dream may not happen in the way that you think or by a certain time. Keep yourself open to the path God is taking you on and the many opportunities and doors you will discover along the way. Keep your intention, and take the steps right there before you. Be grateful before you see it come to pass. Be fruitful in the present moment. Believe and receive what God is sending your way. He does know the way, and it will be a way in which you are transformed as well.

ACTIVATION
DISCOURAGEMENT EXTERMINATOR

When you realize you are feeling discouraged or depressed and struggling to make progress or to do what needs to be done—

DO SOMETHING ELSE!
Sing, Clap, Chant affirmations/scriptures etc. Pray out loud, Dance, Walk outside, Paint, etc.

GO SOMEWHERE ELSE!
Drive to your favorite place, coffee shop, bookstore, museum or park, Take a nap etc.

DO YOUR ROUTINES IN A DIFFERENT WAY!
Drive a different route to work. Take the back roads. Walk downtown instead of the park, or in a whole new location. Buy your morning coffee at a different coffee shop. Eat your breakfast outside instead of at the table. Instead of listening to a podcast, read a book, or draw a picture, etc. Change your exercise. If you usually walk; dance or ride a bike. Sing instead of talking to yourself or to your family/friends. If you normally wear neutral colors; wear bright colors. Change your routine

GIVE YOURSELF A GIFT
What gives you joy? Allow yourself the luxury of giving yourself a gift of time alone, fresh strawberries, a musical instrument to play and sing and dance with, (even if it's just a tambourine), a new set of paints or markers, fun bright china, flowers for the table, a weekend at the river, lake, or ocean, or a fun new outfit. (Give away or throw out old worn-out clothing or clothing you don't like.)

REFRESH YOURSELF.

ACTIVATION
ENCOURAGING WORDS

➤ We must continually change our thinking; upgrade our thinking to the positive.

➤ We can check our focus, our thoughts, to see if they are aligned with where we want to go.

➤ Our focus should be on what we have, not what we don't have, and what we can do, not on what we cannot do.

➤ Make encouragement/affirmation cards.

➤ Make a list of all the affirmations and positive words you want to speak to yourself, scriptures, quotes, etc. that inspire you.

➤ You can use the computer and type on a sheet then cut apart, write on index cards, or make some cards from mixed media sheets:
  • Paint, collage, draw, stamp 2-3 sheets of paper or card stock.
  • Let dry.
  • Cut into business card size or index size cards, whichever you prefer.

➤ Write or glue onto the blank side the encouragement affirmations etc. one per card.

➤ Review these cards daily or one per day.

Check out the free Activation Companion Course for pdfs of quotes and affirmations you can print and cut out to use, along with pdfs of some mixed media sheets.

https://janecookcreate.teachable.com/p/activation-companion-course

8. WHAT IS STOPPING YOU? LACK OF RESULTS?

IS THE LACK of seeing results stopping you?

Progress in growth and development can remain invisible for a time. Even for long periods of time it may appear as if nothing is happening. Some people give up too soon. This slow process can be seen in learning a musical instrument, fitness, learning to speak a foreign language, learning website design; actually in almost everything new there is a time when the learning is not seen. Keep going. Don't judge it. Move on to your next step, you will actually incorporate more than you can tell or know. What you are creating grows within you and it will eventually express itself outwardly as well. It may just be too soon to tell. Even when you have succeeded to activate a dream, you may not see the results you had hoped for. You may not know the results of what you do. We may not see the ripple effects that will go on even past our lives. We must keep going in the embryonic stages of our dream all the way through to the reality. These moments are actually strategic moments when it seems like we are standing still or maybe going backward because it is then we determine if we will eventually be successful. Will you quit or keep going?

> *"Persistence is a slight step ahead of faith.*
> *Every step that persistence takes*
> *has to be followed by a step in faith.*
> *Persistence literally pays. Nothing is truly impossible."*
> —*David Cameron Gikandi*

It will most likely get difficult and a little messy in the midst of the process. Keep going. Don't stop in the middle of the story! The following is some encouragement that I received when I was in Africa for three months. It came to me as a picture in my mind. I saw a half-baked cake.

I felt God speaking:

> *"Your time here is not finished. It is not over.*
> *You have just begun. Do not judge this time yet.*
> *Right now it may look like a runny, gooky mess—*
> *nothing like you envisioned. It is not finished."*

I encourage you as well to keep walking. Keep enduring. God will finish what He has begun. Let Him do in you and through you the whole process. He will take this time for completion and for the purpose and intentions He has for you. He can take all the pieces, the ingredients, and mix them together. It might look like a mess right now. It might look like nothing, but He can take all that and apply the "heat," plus a little time, and it will come together to make a beautiful, delightful, tasty cake for Him and for His glory! You are His delight, a sweet morsel!

Nothing in our lives is lost or wasted. Many things come into convergence and come back around and contribute to our lives. Just because we do not understand the purpose or the why of everything that happens, does not mean that it cannot be used for our benefit. Much of life is a mystery. I think that is why I like collage and mixed-media so much. I like how in mixed-media, little bits and pieces of life, even scraps and trash, can add to the story and the beauty of the work. There is meaning there to be discovered, though it is not obvious and must be searched out or revealed over time. Many mysteries may never be understood as life is far above and beyond our own understanding. We can only seek to know the One who does and is able to understand.

We must trust and leave the results to God. We must just be faithful to do what is in our hearts to do. Just KEEP GOING! Even your journey itself, not just the end result or destination, can inspire others. Even your journey is a legacy. One example of this is seen through the life of Harriet Powers, an African American slave who made applique quilts to record her stories, Bible stories, and African symbols.[1] The applique technique could have been inspired by West African tapestries and passed down to her. Though Harriet was enslaved and forbidden to read or write, she devised a way to have a voice and to keep her memories alive. The story quilts inspired her children, grandchildren, and all those who saw them and learned their meaning. Harriet's journey left a legacy for future generations. Two of her surviving quilts are archived at the National Museum of American History in Washington, D.C. and the Museum of Fine Arts, Boston, MA.

After reading a historical fiction novel, *The Invention of Wings* by Sue Monk Kidd[2], about Harriet Powers and the Grimke' sisters who went from being slave owners to becoming civil rights leaders who spoke out against slavery, I wrote a poem of sorts, which I believe relates to all women in bondage. Our journeys, our stories are our legacies.

Ode to Harriet Powers
Broken and empty with 'lions' in the way,
She escapes and becomes free as she stitches stars,
Creating stories that take her to a different world—
A world of beauty, color, and dancing,
She runs free!
Her freedom leaves a legacy.
—jane

These are actually strategic moments when it seems like we are standing still or maybe going backward because it is then you determine if you will eventually be successful if you quit or keep going.

ACTIVATION
WATCH YOUR MOUTH!

What we speak out of our mouths is so very powerful. When we speak we are creating what we say. We need to speak those things that are positive for ourselves and for others. We need to speak blessings and not curses to ourselves and to others.

Here are some words we need to eliminate from our vocabulary and replace with the positive:

Eliminate: I should...I need to...I'm supposed to —>
Replace with: I choose... I desire... I decide...

Eliminate: I can't —>
Replace with: I can do all things through Christ who strengthens me.

Eliminate: I don't know if I can —>
Replace with: I am committed to...

Eliminate: This and that is wrong or this is a problem —>
Replace with: Where is the opportunity here?

Eliminate: This is hard and difficult —>
Replace with: This is a challenge.

Eliminate: This is impossible —>
Replace with: All things are possible with God.

What other things do you say that you need to create a replacement for?

9. WHAT IS STOPPING YOU? OVERWHELM?

IS OVERWHELM STOPPING you?

Too big of a problem or even too big of a solution can cause feelings of being overwhelmed. Overwhelm leads to paralysis. You may ask yourself, "What could I possibly do to make a difference in this huge problem?" Do you become depressed about the problem? Or just ignore it?

> *"The enemy uses lies to make problems appear*
> *bigger than the solutions we carry."*
> *—Bill Johnson*

One can feel overwhelmed even in just the daily stress of living in today's world. Whether we are seeking to find a creative solution to a problem in our own life or in the lives of others, we must learn to deal with "overwhelm." The solution is a matter of what we are looking at. Overwhelm is really a failure to believe that a divine hand is holding all things together. What we are looking at will grow and become bigger. If we are looking at the problem, it will loom larger and larger until we feel we cannot do anything about it. It's just too big. BUT if we believe in a God who holds the entire universe in His hand, and that He holds all things together, our faith in God grows. He is big enough. He can certainly hold you and give you peace in your personal circumstances and the faith that He can also guide you in your dream to help others in their situations as well. God's love for you is big enough to meet all you need and to equip you for every good work He has put in your heart.

We must fix our eyes on Jesus. He has all wisdom and gives us freely of His wisdom if we ask. When we see a particular problem, when we "see" something and it bothers us, we are most likely to be a part of the solution. God has put that reaction to that thing in us, and He will also give us vision about the solutions and action to be taken. He will show us what our part is to play. No matter how little we feel that part is, we CAN make a difference! Think of the individuals who impacted your life. What was it they did that impacted you? Was it a big thing or a small thing? Was it a simple word or action that made a big difference and affected you in a big way?! Most likely, yes!

We are not designed to carry the problems or burdens of this world. Jesus says to come to Him. His burden is light. His yoke is easy. He will teach us how to rest in Him as we work together with Him. We must give the burden to Him. We must learn to release our concerns to Him each and every day.

Take a moment in your quiet time with Him each day to lift up your care to Him. Visualize Jesus taking that burden from you. I visualize taking my concern and wrapping it up, tying it up in a bundle, and then raising it up to God. His love and His light fill me with joy and peace.

Prayer is

exhaling the Spirit of Man

inhaling the Spirit of God

Give yourself space in your day for quiet and silence to be able to receive from God. Walk in nature, sit quietly, etc. Remind yourself that you, by yourself, are not the answer to the whole problem. You are only required to do your part. All of us together, inspired and empowered by God, will reach the whole world and bring love, joy, creativity, and light into every dark nook and cranny. Just begin to do the things you are motivated to do, no matter if it is small. Give priority to it over other superficial things that are sowing no positive fruit in your life. Ask God every morning what you might do for good in every situation, to help others, and a way, a path, will open up!

One devotion that has encouraged me is from *Come Away My Beloved* by Frances J. Roberts: "Naught will be required of you but obedience. You shall follow the call of the Spirit and not search for the path; for the way will be laid down before you even as you tread. Wherever you stop, there will the path stop also. Whenever you walk in faith, the way will be made clear to you."[1] The path will open up as you walk. So, as you move forward, inch by inch, and foot by foot, you will see where to go next. The beauty of the connections made on the journey will be clear after the fact; as you look back, you will see your beautiful story. Have faith. God knows the way to lead you from where you are to where you need to go! Even more importantly, He will transform you in the process.

As you become aware of overwhelm in your life, you may discover the call to simplify, to set aside things that don't matter and that are not bearing fruit so that you can make more time for those things and people that you care passionately about. As we simplify our lives, not only timewise, but material wise, we are freed to give more and to pursue our dream/vision.

Micah 6:8 NASB reminds us of the simplicity we are to experience.

*"He has told you, O man, what is good; and what
does the Lord require of you but to do justice, to love
kindness, and to walk humbly with your God."*

*"This is what the Lord requires from you: to do what is
right, to love mercy, and to live humbly with your God."*
—God's Word

*"See that justice is done, let mercy be your first
concern, and humbly obey your God."*
—Contemporary English Version

"Lord, I am overwhelmed by needs, expectations,
relationships, and my 'to do' list.
I need an exchange.
I need Your peace for my anxiety,
I need your love and joy for my crankiness and frustration.
I need your "always being present in the moment"
for my schedules and plans and 'shoulds.'
I need Your perspective for my short-sightedness and earthly vision.
I need Your abundance for my poverty mind-set.
I need your absolute confidence and faith in
exchange for my fears and doubts.
I need Your grace for my condemnation and judgment
of myself and others.
I need an exchange.
You have enclosed me behind and before
and laid your hand upon me.
You know. You guide.
I exchange my own way,
my own path for Your perfect way.
I will follow You today.
Amen."
—jane

Your feelings of being overwhelmed, like mine, may come from working on too many projects at one time. My research and reading seem to support the idea that most successful people focus on one thing at a time—one project at a time. They do things sequentially, not simultaneously. I mistakenly believed for years and years that it was a virtue to multi-task, but evidence suggests that this is a poor way of working. Besides jerking the brain back and forth, it wastes lots of time as we try to get refocused on the "other" thing we are doing.

How do we respond to feeling overwhelmed? The only way to overcome is by realizing that we *can* make a difference. We *can* be a part of the solution to the world's problems, but it is done by "doing small things with great love" (Mother Teresa).

Don't look at how big the problem is. Don't make the problem bigger than God, bigger than the solution. Instead of being overwhelmed by problems and by life in general, be overwhelmed by love. Be overwhelmed by God and His love for you. Be overwhelmed by His goodness. Be overwhelmed by this realization:

> *"May Your tender love overwhelm me, O Lord,*
> *for You are my Savior and You keep Your promises."*
> —*Psalm 119:41 TPT*

We are the solution by simply focusing on the ONE. It is about stopping and loving the one in front of us that we change the world.[2]

> *"Stop for the One. Love the One in front of you."*
> —Heidi Baker

> *"What does love look like?"*
> —Heidi Baker

It is about taking some action, some small step, whether donating to feed the hungry, digging a well, or rescuing women and children from the sex trafficking. It's about love in action. It may be a smile, a hug, a listening ear. When we shift from being overwhelmed by the problem and standing on the sidelines doing nothing to becoming a part of the solution, we will move from depression to hope. Focus on the process. Visualize the steps and do those. When we all do that, we *are* changing the world for good!

Let nothing and no one, not even yourself, stop you. Refuse to stop, and you will be unstoppable!

"Be of good cheer. I have overcome the world!"
—Jesus

We need to encourage one another and let people know what is going on for good. We are truly making an impact in the world today. That's how we do it. Each one of us, one at a time, simply stopping and loving and giving. *Together* we make a difference!

"And looking at them Jesus said to them, 'With people this is impossible, but with God all things are possible.'"
—Matthew 19:26 NASB

"Don't fail to do something just because you can't do everything." -Bob Pierce, Stop for the One
"The only people who can change the world are people who want to. And not everybody does."
—Hugh MacLeod

In the *Hole in the Gospel*, Richard Stearns (the CEO of World Vision) reminds us that we as Americans are the rich. We tend to compare ourselves with others. If you make $25,000/year, you are richer than 90% of the world. If you make $50,000/year, you are richer than 99% of the world. There were 6.7 billion people in the world at the time that he wrote the book, and half live on less than $2/day.[3]

When I got back from Africa the first time, I cried. I cried because I had clean water to drink. I cried because I had a shower. I cried because I had a hot shower. I cried when I got in my car to go buy food at Walmart. I was overwhelmed after seeing such need. I think my heart hurt, but I also felt guilty somehow that I live in our big, beautiful country. Then Holy Spirit spoke to me in such a sweet way and told me that I was created for this time and this place. The wealth and the blessings were not all for me, but to share. He trusts me to be accountable and to use what He has put in my hands for the good of others. I wept.

We CAN make a difference. How will you make a difference and bring light into the problem or situation and change the world for yourself, family, friends, community, state, country, or world?

"A bell is no bell until you ring it,
A song is no song until you sing it,
And love in your heart was not put there to stay;
Love isn't love 'till you give it away."
—Oscar Hammerstein II

How could little polymer clay hearts stamped with "loved" on the back make any kind of difference? Yet I felt so impressed to make them and take them on my first trip to Cambodia. I wasn't sure what I would do with the 122 little heart pins. On the nights we went to the Red Light District and to the bars, I took the hearts in my purse and just laid some out on the table. The girls noticed them right away. When I would hand one to them and tell them it was for them and they were loved, they beamed and wanted them pinned on their dresses. I got to hug on them like a momma. We actually started quite a "commotion" at each bar we went to. LOL!

So... What were the "chains" from those little hearts? I don't know, but I do have one story at the last bar we went to. One of the girls really was curious about us and stayed close to me the whole evening. When it was time to go, I said I would be flying back home soon but hoped to return. She said, "Then I not take this heart off until you come back!" Later thinking back on sharing these simple hearts and love, I asked myself:

"What if Vin finds out she is truly loved?"

"What if Vin leaves the sex work and finds out who she really is in Christ and what she is made to do?"

"What if she discovers her purpose and destiny?"

How would this decision affect her baby boy? Her mother? Her friends and co-workers?

How will women learning they are loved by God and have tremendous worth and value to Him, affect the nation?

We are knit together. We may each just be one thread, one link in the chain, but we are connected to something much greater and more beautiful than ourselves. As we link together, we are strong and pursuing love and justice in the world. We are connected to the Kingdom and to God's plan for mankind, and we will see His will done on earth as it is in heaven! We are Jesus' hands and feet. It is up to us to take action.

> *"Every time there is a tragedy or a problem bigger than any solution*
> *we can see, we tend to ask, 'Where is God?' Imagine what would*
> *happen if we stepped up to the plate, each of us said, 'Here is God.*
> *Right here in me; right here in you!' ... It's up to us to call forth our*
> *greatest light and love and be the miracle, right here, right now."*
> —Regina Brett, Be the Miracle

We are ALL giving our lives away, but to what? Besides your inspiration for your dream, there is also a collective desire to have it that David Cameron Gikandi speaks of in *A Happy Pocket Full of Money*.[4] He gives a fresh perspective, a bigger perspective, that there are a group of people asking you and waiting for you to fulfill your desires. There are people praying around the world for just the very thing that you are being inspired to do! YOU are the answer to their prayers. And they are the answer to your prayers as they need what you are wanting to provide. So, when we have a dream or a vision, we need to get excited because that is evidence that someone somewhere is wanting that very thing!

> *"Everybody is an answer to a prayer...*
> *We are all gifts and miracles to each other."*
> —David Cameron Gikandi

The time is *now*. Today is the day! Begin! NOW matters more than any other time in your life, *more* than your past. MORE than what you think you will do tomorrow. Today's decisions determine tomorrow's direction and destiny. Now is truly the only time we have. Time is weird. It is always "now." So, do not put yourself off another day. Take any step, no matter how small, how easy. Do it NOW!

Time
"Is time like a tree?
Can I move from branch to branch in eternity?
As Jesus visited with Moses and Elijah?
God sees our time from beginning to end.
He is outside of time, before and after, eternally.
We are created in His image.
We live and move and breathe in Him.
Can we move between times and realms as well?
After Philip spoke with the eunuch, then believer,
he found himself in another place.
I want to lose myself in Him.
I want to create and play in 'kairos'
In kairos, I become what I am called to be.
I co-create with God.
I want to be aware of life every minute, every day.
In creativity, I am freed from normalcy."
—jane

(The Greek word "chronos" measures time in second, minutes,
days, years. "Kairos" measures time, the best moments of life.
It measures the quality of time, not minutes,
but measures moments. quora.com)

"Let's stir ourselves up and each other to love and good deeds."
—Hebrews 10:24

"So we are convinced that every detail of our lives is continually
woven together to fit into God's perfect plan of bringing good into
our lives, for we are His lovers who have been called to fulfill His
designed purpose. For He knew all about us before we were born and
He destined us from the beginning to share the likeness of His Son."
—Romans 8:28-29

Let's seek to do what Kris Vallotton encourages us to do in Culture of Honor:

*"Pour gas on the fire of dreams.
Pour water on the flames of fear."*

We want to do this for ourselves, but we must also encourage each other, stirring up the fire in each other. We are not in competition with each other, we are working together, each in our place and plan. We must help extinguish the fear in each other by love and support. There is not only enough room for all of us, every single person on the planet has a place and a purpose and is so needed. Each of us is irreplaceable, never again in history repeatable. Let us treasure the gold in each person we meet.

*"Discover creative ways to encourage others and
to motivate them toward acts of compassion,
doing beautiful works as expressions of love."
—Hebrews 10:24 TPT*

*"Our stories are meant to mingle,
rubbing against one another like
iron sharpening iron. When that happens, sparks ignite. The place
of testing, conviction, and hope born of past trials and victories,
become fertile soil for the next seed of glory to bear fruit."
—Lou Engle*

*"As we let our own light shine, we unconsciously
give others permission to do the same."
—Marianne Williamson*

ACTIVATION
GAS & WATER

"Pour gas on the fire of dreams.
Pour water on the flames of fear."
—Kris Vallotton

> Think of someone today who could use some encouragement about pursuing their dreams.
> Call them up. Text them. Take them to lunch.
> Encourage them to share and to talk about their dream with you.
> Listen for any fears and give them "in courage"ing words.
> You may even want to pray for them.
> Share what you are learning.
> Maybe share a copy of this book.

I hope I have ignited a spark in you! My message is "I am average. I am a normal, regular person." I know how to do a lot of things in an average way. I am curious about lots of things and love to learn continuously. I am a learner. I'm no genius or an extremely super-talented person. Have you ever read or heard someone's story, their journey and success, and felt so depressed instead of encouraged? That somehow they could do these great, amazing things, but you couldn't, so instead of being encouraged you felt "less than?" My prayer is that my writing as a regular, ordinary woman, virtually unknown and still in the process and on the journey of following and taking action on my dream, helps you to see that you truly *are* enough to do what you desire. My message is that you do not have to be someone better or more special than others to pursue your dreams.

You just have to understand that you *are* an original, unique combination of experiences, background, skills, gifts, and perspective that no one else can have. You are fully equipped and prepared to do today, the opportunity of this present moment, to take that step to begin or to continue. Just by living your dream, you will inspire others. You and me, ordinary people, living out our dreams. Do not think your dream is for someone else to do or that someone else could do it better. No! Someone else has their own dream to do in their own unique way. They cannot do your dream like you can. It is time to take your dreams out of hiding. It is time to take out those dreams that were stashed away for later. It is time to bring them out into the light so they can be seen. It is time to begin. As you take each step, the next one will open up, and the next and the next, until one day you turn around and see the beautiful path that has taken you to a place where your dream is manifest, and you realize that it will continue to grow, change, and expand in the future as you continue to seize the opportunities of the present moment.

At first it really bothered me that I am not farther along in this vision to be able to say, "Look at the 10,000s of women we have helped escape from sex trafficking," or "Look at the artisan businesses and the gross sales we have made that are helping us start more groups and support more women around the world." Then I realized once again that I am not in any way saying I am doing things perfectly, and you should do as I have done. My being in the process is the very thing that takes down any barriers between us so that you can truly see that YOU are enough, *more* than enough to accomplish all the good plans and purposes God has for you.

What *you* are called to do is important and can impact the world for good. So, take the small steps, use what's in your hands, be who you are, and get moving! Do not be hung up on how "good" you are or are not at whatever it is. That is not the pre-requisite to your purpose. Besides, you only have to be yourself, and you are the best one to do that. So, no competition there. Start! Get moving! Remember Newton's 1st law from school, "Objects in motion tend to stay in motion." Once a task has begun, it is easier to keep moving forward. Stop talking about it. DO IT! It is only in the action that momentum continues. People are waiting! Burn with passion and bear much fruit! Be who you are created to be, where you are supposed to be, doing what you are passionate about.

The very fact that you have that dream/vision reveals that there is a reason you do—because there are people waiting for you to bring them what it is you are desiring to do! Your desires and dreams are not just for you, but for others. We are interconnected and need one another.

"A", a single-mother of two children, found herself working in the bar/brothel just to be able to provide for them. One night a group came into the bar and talked with her. Before they left, one of them asked if they could pray for her. She told her that she believed that she would be getting a new job opportunity very soon. She gave her a cross necklace. "A" had been crying out to God for a different job. She was so worried that her son would soon discover what she had to do to provide for them. Not too long after this word of encouragement to her, another person who had gotten to know her over a period of time, told her that their organization was starting a new artisan group for women who would be learning jewelry design. "A" was very excited to hear about it and made the decision to be the first woman to join the group. While God had put on my heart to use my jewelry skills to help women create sustainable income for themselves and their children, "A" was crying out to God for help. My dream, your dream, is not all about us; it is for others.

Give all your gifts away in service and in love to the world. People are waiting!

"Two great tasks of a human life: to find
ourselves and to lose ourselves."
—John Izzo, PhD, The 5 Secrets You Must Discover

We are free to be ourselves. We do not have to be super talented, skilled, intelligent, or wealthy people, although we may be. We are unique just as we are. We are all special in our own ways. Your uniqueness is yours alone to bring. We can be just ordinary people who by action and by doing what our hearts lead us to, become extraordinary! It happens in the action with courage and faith. The extraordinary is in the ACTION. We all have dreams, desires, visions, and ideas, but what is it that makes things amazing? It is in the *action* of it. It is in actually taking the steps that bring those things in your heart out into reality for the world. And as we do, the world changes!

"The ordinary + extra attention = the extraordinary."
—Austin Kleon

"How strange is the lot of us mortals! Each of us is here for
a brief sojourn; for what purpose he knows not, though he
sometimes thinks he senses it. But without deeper reflection
one knows from daily life that one exists for other people ...
a hundred times every day I remind myself that my inner
and outer life are based on the labors of other men, living
and dead, and that I must exert myself in order to give in the
same measure as I have received and am still receiving."
—Albert Einstein

CALL TO ACTION

SO, DEAR CREATIVE World Changers, let's encourage one another. The world needs us. We need each other. Every one of us has a part, a place in God's big, beautiful world. Reach out. Stretch out beyond yourself in love for the good of others. Every single problem our world faces today has creative solutions. Once you *see* a creative solution, you will climb over, under, or through, and tell any excuse or obstacle to move! As we each give our "average," "ordinary" selves out to the world, extraordinary, amazing things happen! The world is waiting!

And as my friend Charlie told me before my second trip to Cambodia:

"Hands Up! Enjoy the Ride!"

I pictured myself on a roller coaster ride with all the wild ups and downs and curves with my hands up laughing and screaming my head off! He was so right. I raised my hands many, many times during the challenges of this journey and repeated, "Hands Up! Enjoy the Ride!"

I added my gratitude and thankfulness to God for the opportunity to see the vision fulfilled. Enjoy the journey, even those steep downs and sharp unexpected turns. Have faith that the journey is not over and much is yet to come! Good things are just around the bend!

"More important than talent, strength, or knowledge is the ability to laugh at yourself and enjoy the pursuit of your dreams."
—Amy Grant, Singer, Songwriter

ACTIVATION
HANDS UP!

> Picture yourself on a roller coaster with steep hills and wild turns and twists, the roller coaster of life, the roller coaster of your journey to see your dream fulfilled.
> Raise your hands and say, "Hands up! Enjoy the Ride!" Release. Let go! Even when things get crazy, I actually raise my hands and say out loud, "Hands up! Enjoy the Ride!"
> It reminds me to release things to God and to be grateful and thankful for all that has happened already and every good thing that is happening presently.
> I will give thanks in the difficult times as well.
> I thank God that He is in me. I will seize every opportunity before me.

You have completed a first step. You finished this book, *What's Stopping You? Face Your Fears, Ignite Your Passion and Activate Your Dreams*. You did it! Now you see that it is really not "what" is stopping you, but "who," and the "who" is you.

That's the good thing, because no one and nothing can stop you, but you, and you can decide today that you are unstoppable! What green light do you have? Don't look all the way down the road, waiting for every light ahead to turn green; just go through the first one.

You are unstoppable!

I will be heading back to Cambodia. Where are you headed? No one people, group, or person is more important than another in the world. You may be headed next door, to the nursing home, to your grandkids, to the hospital, to work, or home. Every person is important. Begin your dream today, right where you are, with the people around you, with the opportunities that you have, with LOVE.

We must recognize the importance and significance of the *one*. Even in the writing of this book, I have no idea if it will get into the hands of many people. At one point, with my stacks of paper all around, I almost quit. I almost allowed doubt and the critic in my head to stop me from finishing. Then I reminded myself, and I kept reminding myself all through the process, that even if my writing only helps one person it is so very worth it. If one person is encouraged to take action on their dream/vision, and they reach many, many people with their vision, then it is so worth it. That is my desire for YOU! My hope for you is that you go out and do ridiculously, wildly amazing things that impact the world!

"Do all the good you can, in all the ways you can, in all the places you can, at all the times you can, as long as you ever can."
—John Wesley

The light is green.
What are you waiting for?
You are unstoppable!

ACTIVATION
YOU ARE UNSTOPPABLE!

> Have someone take a picture of you in your "UNSTOPPABLE" position. Have fun with it!
> Print it out on your computer.
> Cut it out. Set it aside while you prepare the rest of the mixed media piece.
> Write or stamp all nine obstacles (fear, failure, procrastination, age, no results, not enough, life difficulties, and overwhelm) on strips of torn scraps of paper. (colored, white, painted, magazine, newsprint, etc.) You may want to write out your specific fears, specific difficulties etc.
> Glue these strips of obstacles that are trying to stop you from seeing your dream come true, into a mountain shape. You may want to add paint.
> Glue the picture of 'Unstoppable You' on top of the mountain.
> Type out or cut out the words from a magazine, stamp, write or paint these words:

"I AM UNSTOPPABLE!"

> You may add paint etc. Whatever you wish.
> Hang it up where you will see it daily.
> You may want to take a pic of it to use it in your phone as wallpaper or print it off smaller.

Okay Creative World Changers, no matter where you are in the process of your vision right now, you are on your way. You have read the book. You are doing the activations. You are overcoming obstacles to your dream. You are facing your fears. You have taken some action steps. Appreciate and be grateful for each small step. Your passion is ignited. You are realizing that your dream is not just about you, but about others, and they are waiting and praying for you to do it; to bring your dream into the world in a way only you can! You have momentum going. Keep moving forward.

I would encourage you to share this book with a friend or a book club to discuss the book and encourage each other to go for it! I encourage you to go to the free Activation Companion Course to watch the bonus videos, listen to the bonus audios, and to DO the activations to move your dream into reality! https://janecookcreate.teachable.com/p/activation-companion-course

What would our world look like if we all believed our lives are created for purpose and for good? What would our world look like if each of us connected to our Creator God and awakened to our powerful, unique selves? What would our world look like if we all took action and followed our own unique dreams and passions? We are each a part of a bigger story!

I am excited for you and would love to continue our journeys together. I want to hear YOUR story! I want to celebrate with you when you take your first step toward your dream or you see your vision come into reality.

Contact me here at https://iuwe4good.com/ and share your dream/vision.

What obstacles were stopping you? What small first step did you take? How did you get the momentum going? What is your next step? Declaring your creative dream helps to make it "real."

I would also like to invite you to join the iuwe4good community to connect, support, and encourage others who are also pursuing their vision/dream for the good of others. We need a community of creatives with hearts of love to see dreams and passions fulfilled. iuwe4good is a safe space to share/connect/and inspire.

We are "Better Together." Let's share together our journeys.

To join us, visit *https://iuwe4good.com/join/*

> *"If you want to go fast, go alone;*
> *but if you want to go far, go together."*
> —*African Proverb*

If you have already started and are actively pursuing your vision/dream, would you connect with me at https://iuwe4good.com/? Share with me what you are doing and how you are helping people through creativity. How are you changing the world? I will reach out to you to get more information if I choose to highlight your story and possibly interview you, share your website, video, product link, or business on my website, so we can encourage even more people to get up and get moving to see their creativity become reality through their vision/dream.

"Creative World Changers," contact me here today!
https://iuwe4good.com
I can't wait to hear YOUR story!
TODAY is the day!
YOU ARE UNSTOPPABLE!

P.S. To reach a dream is not the end. It is only the beginning. Remember that sometimes we think we know where we are going and then find out there is more to the story. Never limit yourself or what God may want to do through you. There are continuous dreams and journeys. Keep allowing yourself to imagine, create, and seek.

The publishing of this book is in the wake of the covid-19 virus. The message of this book is not moot; it is even *more*, not less, relevant and needed. Now more than ever, each one of us needs to bring hope, love, compassion, and connection with one another into our world. Do not let anything keep you from pursuing your dreams. This is a time to rise up, to shine, to stand strong, and go forward. It is a time to "think outside the box" and bring creative solutions into our world. There is a way to accomplish all that you are called to do. Do not be discouraged or overwhelmed. Take your small step that is before you today. The effect is in the action!

> *"I have been impressed with the urgency of doing.*
> *Knowing is not enough; we must apply.*
> *Being willing is not enough; we must do."*
> —Leonardo da Vinci

My sweetener packet this morning said, ***"Imagine. Do. Repeat."***
I love that! Life is a beautiful journey. Life is an adventure!
I want to hear about yours!

I wish you the greatest success. Remember that God's plans are above and beyond all that you could ever ask, hope, think, or imagine! (Ephesians 3:20)

Go for it! Celebrate each small step along the way, and KEEP GOING!

—jane

ACTIVATION
IUWE4GOOD

> ➤ Do you want to be surrounded with a community of love, encouragement, and support?
> ➤ Do you desire to use your creativity 4 good in the world for others?
> ➤ Do you desire to be a World Changer and to make a difference by doing what is in your heart and soul to do?
> ➤ Do you seek to live creatively inspired and empowered?
> ➤ Do you desire to connect with others who are making a difference in the world?
> ➤ iuwe4good is a community of average, ordinary people who are living extraordinary lives. People who experience discouragement, overwhelm, and fear but overcome and seek to live life to the fullest in each moment. People like you.
> ➤ I would love to invite you to join the iuwe4good Creative World Changers community. Help us build an amazing creative community as we share life together as we follow our dreams and passions to impact the world today!
> ➤ Join the iuwe4good community at https://www.iuwe4good.com, a place for you to connect with other Creative World Changers, to encourage, support, and collaborate as you grow your dreams.
> ➤ You will hear testimonies of their successes and struggles and have the opportunity to share yours.
> ➤ What is in your heart and what is happening 4good through you in the world? No matter how big or how small, you are making a difference!

Prayer
"Lord, make us instruments of Thy peace;
Where there is hatred, let us sow love;
Where there is injury, pardon;
Where there is doubt, faith;
Where there is despair, hope;
Where there is darkness, light;
And where there is sadness, joy."
—Francis of Assisi

ACTIVATION
YOUR JOURNEY TO KNOW GOD

I started the book off speaking to you honestly about God and His impact on my life. I would love to hear about your journey to know God. You can contact me at https://www.janecookcreate.com/contact-jane/

These questions are for you to see what God might be doing in your life.

1. When have you heard from God in the past?
2. What has happened in your life that is not explainable in the natural?
3. When have you sensed God's Presence or God's love for you?
4. Is there a person in your life who knows God?
5. Is there a person in your life who prays for you?
6. Have you felt a desire to know God? Or to follow Jesus? Why or Why not?
7. What do you think God would say to you right now?
8. Where are you on your journey of life?
9. Where are you on your journey to know yourself?
10. Where are you on your journey with God?

When we know our Creator we have a lot of 'inside' information about life and about ourselves; who we are and why we are here. We also have access to infinite wisdom, knowledge, understanding, creativity, solutions, miracles, faith, joy, hope, peace, stability, and love beyond ourselves. I would invite you that if you do not have a relationship with God through Jesus, to ask Him to come into your life. Jesus is truly the way to the Father. He has paid the price for you and opens the door wide for you to enter His kingdom and all that He is and all that He has. He loves and adores you. You can ask Jesus to come into your life by yourself, or with others. Just talk to Him. If you would like to talk to someone about it, ask a believer who is a friend or someone you trust. You may also email me. I'd love to rejoice with you and encourage you on your journey. Spend time praying, talking to Him, listening to Him, and reading His Word. I highly recommend starting in John, the New Testament, Psalms, and Proverbs, and to read the Bible in an easy to read translation that you can understand. Holy Spirit will lead and guide you into truth and a deeper relationship with God, Your Creator and Father.

THANK YOU FOR READING MY BOOK!

I really appreciate having this opportunity to share with
you my journey and to encourage you on yours.
I would so love to hear some feedback on the book–whatever helped
you or any questions you might have.

Please leave me a review on Amazon
to let me know what you thought of the book.

Thank you so much!

jane cook

Be sure to check out the FREE Activation Companion Course for pdfs
of the activations, bonus material, videos, and audios.

ACKNOWLEDGMENTS

IT HAS BEEN 17 years since the seed of this vision to encourage women in their creativity began to grow and to develop and now has become a non-profit organization called Empowered Women Create, to help women around the world in a more powerful way by connecting with other women who care about women, freedom, and oppression.

This book is dedicated to my husband, Kevin, who has always believed in and supported me in a way that continues to surprise me. He has *skin in the game*! …and to my amazing daughters, Melissa and Sarah, who support me in my "creative" ideas even when it costs them something as well. To my wonderful grandkids who continually inspire me to stay young, fun, and creative – Jacob, Eli, Kylee, Caleb, Claire, Chloe, and Lexi. To my Mom and Dad who gave me such a wonderful, loving, and supportive foundation for my life. To Suzann who has been a constant support and sounding board for me personally and for all my "wild" ideas. I also want to recognize Heidi Baker who profoundly impacted my life with her life as a "laid down lover of Christ" and an example of what it looks like to "Stop for the One and to Love the One."

Thank you to the beautiful women who helped me with the launch of this book and their love and support. Each one of you has inspired me and is lighting up the world. Thank you for your friendship and saying, "Yes!" to be a part of the vision: Scottye Adkins, Vicki Beckham, Donna Bollinger, Melissa Bollinger, Margaret Bullock, Yvonne Carter, Sandi Chamberlain, Theda Childers, Jacque Cooper, Melanie Coppenger, Dayle Doroshow, Jackie Green, Sara Grim, Anna Grim, Christy Hall, Jessica Harmon, Vickie Harper, Lorri Hernandez, Shari House, Christina Jackson, Karen LaBrot, Connie Lee, Suzann Lynch, Marty Lynch, Sarah McFarland, Karon Murphy, Vicki Patterson, Catherine Roux, Diane Schnabel, Kathryn Senter, Deborah Sharon, and Kathleen Wichterman. Thank you to Pastor Bill Miller and his wonderful support and willingness to be a reference for many of my ventures! Thank you to Jackie Green for being such an encouraging friend who has been with me from the beginning when my dream was just an impression. Thank you to Sky Nuttall (my amazing and encouraging editor), to Sara, Deborah, and Connie for helping with the proofreading, to Laurette Willis for your support and endorsement, and other friends and family too numerous to name!

And most of all I want to acknowledge the God of the Universe who cares for and loves each one of us and chooses to share His amazing creativity with us to partner with Him by faith, imagination, and creativity to bring the unseen into the seen; to bring His Kingdom of Love on earth as it is in Heaven.

BOOK DISCUSSION QUESTIONS

INTRODUCTION

1. Do you believe that you are genuinely unique by God's design?
2. Are you happy to be you? Free to be you?
3. Who do you feel most comfortable with? Why?
4. Is there a dream that has continued in your heart?
5. What do you need to believe about yourself to pursue your dream?
6. Is there a voice telling you that you cannot do something? What is it? How do you respond to Vincent van Gogh's quote, *If you hear a voice within you say, 'You cannot paint,' then by all means paint, and that voice will be silenced.*
7. Do you feel average or ordinary? Does that rule out being extraordinary?
8. How would you describe your background and what part does it or has it played toward your dream?

I. TIPS FOR THE JOURNEY

#1 Be Curious
9. What are you interested in?
10. Share your answer for one of the nine questions.
11. Did you write out what a day looks like when your vision is fulfilled? Did you record and listen to it?
    How did it make you feel? Can you see it?

#2 Invest in Your Interest
12. Have you invested in yourself? How? How else can you?
13. Who can you learn from?

#3 The Next Step to Give Your Gift to the World
14. What step did you take to do this?

#4 Take the Steps. Ask. Seek. Push on the Door
15. What is you "impossible" next step?

#5 Keep Learning. Be Open. Think 'Outside the Box'

16. What does the quote by Einstein mean? *Imagination is more important than knowledge.*

17. Where are you 'outside the box?'

#6 Make a Greater Commitment

18. Do you have a bigger commitment to make to see your dream become real?

19. What will it require?

#7 Shift Gears

20. What convergences have taken place in your life?
    What things in the past have come back around to the present?

#8 Follow Your Heart. Take Action

21. Where has your heart taken you?

22. Do you believe you are here for a purpose that impacts others?

#9 Take Fearless Action

23. How has your vision changed along the way?

24. Do you have a fearless leap to take? Or have you taken it? What was it?

#10 It Takes Time

25. Have you had to wait?

26. What has your timing been like?

27. How did you persevere?

#11 Don't Miss the Opportunities Along the Way

28. What other opportunities have happened on the way to your dream?

#12 Don't Let Your 'Limitations' Keep You From Pursuing Your Vision

29. What do you feel like are your limitations?

30. How have you overcome them?

31. Were they really limitations?

32. Did they keep you from your dream?

#13 Sacrifice – Not Only for You but for Your Family

33. What sacrifice is involved for you and your loved ones for you to fulfill your dream?

#14 Others

34. Are others involved with your dream? How is that going? (positive and negative)

#15 Stuff Happens. Can You Keep Going?

35. What difficulties have you faced?

36. How have you kept going?

#16 Make Time for Quiet

37. Do you take time to get quiet in the morning to connect with God?

38. What ways work well for you to do this?

39. How do you care for your body? Soul? Spirit?

#17 Expansion Requires Stretching. You Will Feel It. Keep Going.

40. Were you or are you stretched in the process?

41. What positive result comes from stretching?

#18 Be Willing to Shift

42. What shifts have taken place from your original idea/dream?

43. Were you able to go with it?

#19 Do the Work

44. How are you doing on the "work" part of your dream?

45. How do you keep yourself activated?

II. ENCOURAGEMENT FOR YOUR JOURNEY

46. Do you see how the ordinary becomes extraordinary when we take action? How?
47. What small thing is in your hands?
48. Do you see how some small thing or some small act by one person can impact the world in a huge way as in *The Butterfly Effect*?
49. What "chains" have you experienced in your life? Share your written and drawn chain from the activation.

#20 Everything You Do Matters

50. What did you think of Admiral McRaven's part of his speech that said, "…if everyone changed the lives of just 10 people, and each of those changed the lives of another 10 people etc. then in 5 generations or 125 years, you will have changed the lives of 800 million people."
51. Have you changed the lives of 10 people? Small things count!
52. What does Proverb 13:23 mean to you?
   Abundant food is in the fallow ground of the poor.
53. What does the Haitian Proverb mean to you?
   We see from where we stand.

#21 It Takes Action, No Matter How Small, to Begin the Chain

54. What easy step do you take to get going?
55. Why do small steps matter?

III. WHAT'S STOPPING YOU?

#1 Fear

56. What fears are stopping you?
57. What do you think about the comment to just "do it anyway?"
58. What does David Cameron Gikandi's quote, *Worry is a self-fulfilling prophecy,* mean? How has worry affected you in the past?
59. What helps you to overcome fear?

60. How does love overcome fear? What stories or example do you have of love overcoming fear?

#2 Failure

61. Have you failed? What did you learn? Did you keep trying? Did you succeed?

#3 Age

62. Do you think age has kept you from pursing your dream? Either too young or too old?
63. What do you think about Anne Lander's comment to the person saying they were too old to go back to school?

#4 Not Enough

64. Do you think that you are not enough or that you don't have enough? What is it? Why?
65. What does God say about that? Have you asked Him?

#5 Procrastination

66. What are the "sly little foxes" in your life? How will you catch them?
67. What is the "secret ingredient" of activation?
68. Do you live like William Borden with "no reserves, no retreats, no regrets?" How can you?

#6 Life

69. Share what season of life you are in.
70. Do you feel like life is stopping you from moving forward with your dream?
71. What CAN you do today in this season of your life?

#7 Discouragement

72. What did you learn from Joseph's life?
73. How did he persevere to accomplish his destiny and purpose?

#8 No Results

74. How do you keep going when you do not see results?

75. What encourages you?

#9 Overwhelm

76. What must be our focus to overcome the overwhelm?

77. Can you make a difference?

78. How can you "pour gas on the fire of dreams, and water on the flames of fear?'

IV. CALL TO ACTION

79. What action are you taking now?

80. Do you believe that you are the only thing stopping you?

81. What green light do you see?

82. How are you inspired by this book? What helped you the most?

83. Who can you encourage to go for their dream? How will you encourage them?

NOTES

Chapter 1 – Be Curious

1. Rigby, Amy. "How to Boost Your Creativity the Einstein Way – With Combinatory Play." 14 January. 2019. <https://blog.trello. com/combinatory-play-boost-creativity/>
2. "Beethoven's Surprisingly Simple Habit for Creative Breakthroughs." Sparring Mind Newsletter. https://www. sparringmind.com/creative-ideas/

Chapter 5 – Outside the Box

1. Lasneski, Lyn. https://yourcreativegenius.org/
2. Evernote Team. "Albert Einstein's Unique Approach to Thinking." Evernote.com/blog. https://evernote.com/blog/ einsteins-unique-approach-to-thinking/
3. Irwin, Nicola. "The Surprisingly Creative Side of Winston Churchill." Independent.ie. 21 November. 2017. https://www. independent.ie/world-news/and-finally/the-surprisingly-creative-side-of-winston-churchill-36339702.html
4. Gelb, Michael J. *How to Think Like Leonardo da Vinci*. New York, New York: Bantam Dell, 1998

Chapter 16 – Make Time for Quiet

1. Willis, Laurette. PraiseMoves®. https://praisemoves.com/ and https://www.youtube.com/user/Fit4Christ

Chapter 17 – Keep Going

1. Korzonek, Michal. "Minimalist Journaling: A Fun and Effective Tool for Tremendous Habit Change." 13 June, 2018. Medium Blog.

Section II – Encouragement for Your Journey

1. Andrews, Andy. *The Butterfly Effect: How Your Life Matters.* United States, Thomas Nelson, 2010.
2. *The Boy Who Harnessed the Wind.* Directed by Chiwetel Ejiofor. 2019.
3. "Admiral McRaven's Life Lesson #9: Sing In The Mud." YouTube. The University of Texas at Austin, 18 June. 2014. https://www.youtube.com/watch?v=XiZpii6983s. McRaven, Admiral Harry.

Chapter 20 – Everything You Do Matters

1. "Admiral Harry McRaven Addresses the University of Texas at Austin Class of 2014." YouTube. The University of Texas at Austin, 23 May. 2014.
2. Main, Bruce. *Why Jesus Crossed the Road.* Tyndale House Publishers, 2010

Chapter 21 – It Takes Only One Small Action

1. Clear, James. https://jamesclear.com/
2. Hardy, Darren. *The Compound Effect.* Vanguard Press, 2010.

3. Tracy, Brian. *Focal Point*. United States, Amacom, 2002.

Section III – What's Stopping You?

Chapter 1 – Fear?

1. Williamson, Marianne. *A Return to Love*. United States, HarperCollins, 1992.
2. *Secret Life of Walter Mitty*. Directed by Ben Stiller. 2013.
3. *Susie's Hope*. Directed by Jerry Rees. 2013.
4. Roberts, Frances J. *On the High Road of Surrender*. Barbour Books. 1987

Chapter 3 – Age?

1. Dan Waldschmidt. "This List Proves You're Never Too Old to Do Something Amazing." Edgy Conversations. Business Insider. 13 March. 2014. https://www.businessinsider.com/100-amazing-accomplishments-achieved-at-every-age-2014-3
2. Bennett, Sam. *Get It Done*. Ann Landers' story. New World Library. 2014.

Chapter 4 – Not Enough?

1. Twist, Lynne. *The Soul of Money*. New York, New York: W.W. Norton & Company. 2003.

Chapter 5 – Procrastination?

1. William Borden. In Wikipedia. Retrieved from https://en.m.wikipedia.org/wiki/William_Whiting_Borden

Chapter 7 – Discouragement?

1. Carnegie, Dale. *Public Speaking.* General Board of Young Men's Christian Org. 1926

Chapter 8 – Lack of Results?

1. Lyons, Mary E. *Stitching Stars: The Story Quilts of Harriet Powers.* Atheneum. 1993
2. Kidd, Sue Monk. *The Invention of Wings.* United States. Penguin Books. 2014.

Chapter 9 – Overwhelm?

1. Roberts, Frances J. *Come Away My Beloved.* King's Farspan, Inc. 1970.
2. Baker, Heidi. https://www.irisglobal.org/
3. Stearns, Richard. *Hole in Our Gospel.* Thomas Nelson. 2009.
4. Gikandi, David Cameron. *A Happy Pocket Full of Money.* Hampton Roads Publishing Co. 2008.

ABOUT THE AUTHOR

JANE COOK IS the President and Founder of Empowered Women Create.

She is a mother of 2 beautiful girls, MiMa to 7 outrageously wonderful grandkids, and wife to a tremendously supportive husband of 44 years. She took early retirement as a school teacher to pursue her art full-time. She has worked in polymer clay and other jewelry mediums for over 25 years.

Jane opened and ran the Oasis Christian Bookstore and Holy Grounds Coffee shop for 10 years and sold it to continue her current journey to help women vulnerable to poverty and undesirable employment to create sustainable income for themselves and their children, as well as giving them the joy and freedom of pursuing their own dreams and visions.

She loves to encourage women to pursue their creativity and their dreams. Jane also gives workshops in polymer clay, mixed-media, and creativity. The journey has taken her from Bonne Terre, MO, to Africa, to Haiti, to Thailand, to Fiji, and to Cambodia.

You can follow Jane on her blog at janecookcreate.com, connect with Empowered Women Create at empoweredwomencreate.org, and be a part of the creative community at iuwe4good.com

MY PRAYER FOR YOU

"God, I thank You for Your amazing good plans and purposes for each and every person reading this book. May they come to know that they CAN do all things through You; that they CAN see their beautiful dreams come to life. NOTHING is too big, too hard, or too complicated for You. Your power in them is more than enough for all that they are called to be or to do. With You ALL things are possible. You are so faithful. You are so good. Every good and perfect gift comes down from You the Father of lights, who never changes.

May each one see You. May they hear Your voice, follow Your way and Your path, in Your time. May each one come to realize that their key time is the present moment. They have enough time. They have enough resources. They have an abundance for every good work. They have enough connections. They have enough energy, love, and compassion. They are enough. You are working in them to finish the good work that You started in them. (Philippians 1:16)

May each one blossom as they take fearless action to do what they are called to do in their lives and to be the people they are called to be. May each one come to see Your great love for them and the incredible value and worth they are to You. May they come to see how wonderfully unique they are and seek to live each precious moment of their lives fully empowered and equipped for every good work. Open their eyes to see that they are indeed the World Changers! May they see the 'one' in front of them. Amen!" —jane

Made in the USA
Monee, IL
06 April 2021